THE OLD FIRE STATION

1881-2018 A HISTORY

HELEN CHADNEY, JEANETTE HOILE, BRYON FEAR,
MALCOLM WOODMAN

LOTTERY FUNDED

This book was commissioned by the South London Theatre Building Preservation Trust Ltd and the Heritage Lottery Fund. It has been created on behalf of South London Theatre by the following people:

Helen Chadney – Co-editor and writer
Jeanette Hoile – Co-editor, project manager, researcher and writer
Bryon Fear – Designer, photographer, illustrator and writer
Stephen Oxford – Researcher and writer
Malcolm Woodman – Writer
Chris Bennett – Archival adviser and collator of reproduction permissions
Phil Gammon – Photographer
Carole Coyne – Liaison with HLF
Geoff Barlow – Print adviser

ACKNOWLEDGEMENTS

We are indebted to Karen Butti, of Thomas Ford and Partners, for her permission to use the Conservation Management Plan, and for her generous and invaluable support throughout the project. Many thanks to Paul Sharrock and Simon McCormack, Terry Jones, Visual Collection Manager, Jane Rugg, Curator, and Elena Lewendon, Curator, of the London Fire Brigade Museum for their advice and assistance, as well as Amanda Wright, Parish Administrator at St Luke's Church, West Norwood, Len Reilly, Archivist at the Lambeth Archives, Jeremy Smith, London Metropolitan Archives, Alasdair Brooks, British Red Cross Archives and Museum, Bob Freshwater, www.britishtelephones.com, English Heritage Archive, The Canterbury Auction Galleries and Sarah Foden, Archivist, Cadbury Archive, Mondelēz International.

Thanks are also due to the following people for their contributions and assistance:

Roger Barton, Caroline Beckett, Keefe Browning, Bob Callender, Charlie Cheetham, Chaz Doyle, Brian Fretwell, Bill Hickin, Anton Krause, Naomi Liddle, Geoff Lill, Matthew Lyne, Ann Mattey, Mike Mattey, John Nadal, Ann Parnell-McGarry, Colin Stokes, Lisa Thomas and Val Williams.

CONTENTS

INTRODUCTION

A history playing supporting roles

A building is not merely bricks and mortar. Every building has a presence, a sense of identity and a character – one that is informed by its purpose; its size; the materials from which it is formed; where it sits in the landscape and its relationship to the neighbouring buildings and structures; and, not unimportantly, the people that use it and are associated with it.

The Old Fire Station was built during the reign of Queen Victoria and completed in 1882. It stands on the site of the Great North Wood which once stretched from Selhurst & West Wickham in the south, to Deptford on the Thames in the north. The hill on which the Old Fire Station stands was at the heart of this ancient territory first appearing in written records in 1272.

The Great North Wood became truncated both in size and name due to the population influx of the industrial revolution, but its once majestic presence can still be felt throughout South London: Norwood, Forest Hill, Penge (edge of wood) and Honor Oak.

Population growth in the capital necessitated improved public protection and the Metropolitan Fire Brigade was created. Due to its location and height in the landscape the Lower Norwood site was chosen for a new fire station. Designed by noted architect Robert Pearsall, it is not only a building but a work of art. Built with a Victorian gothic aesthetic, it was designed to keep people safe and its iconic watch tower is testament to that original purpose.

In the past 136 years the building has performed many roles, from fire station to community space; nurses' quarters and parish hall; to its current use as a theatre. It has shaped the lives of many, and those many have, in turn, reshaped the building.

This is the history of the Old Fire Station: a story of a building that was designed to protect the lives of the people of South London and how, when it was most in need, those people returned the favour.

Opposite: Knight's Hill, The Great North Wood. (John Rocque, 1792)

CHAPTER ONE

Early life of the Old Fire Station 1881-1916

"Fire!

This startling cry aroused me one night and, rushing to the window, I could just perceive a dull, red glare in the northern sky which, even as I gazed, became vivid and threw some chimneys near at hand into strong relief. A fire, undoubtedly, and not far distant.

The scene is weird and striking: the intense glare, the shooting flames which dart viciously out and upwards, the white and red faces of the crowd kept back by the busy police, the puff and clank of the engines, the rushing and hissing of the water, the roar of the fire, and the columns of smoke which in heavy, sulky masses hang gloating over the blazing building. The bright helmets of the firemen are glinting everywhere, close to the already tottering wall, on the summit of the adjacent buildings, which are already smoking. Lost on ladders, amid smoke, they pour a torrent of water on the burning and seething premises. Above all the monotonous "puff, puff" of the steamer is heard, and a buzz of

admiration ascends from the attentive, silent crowd suddenly arises a yell – a wild, unearthly cry which almost makes one's blood run cold, even in that atmosphere. A tremor seizes us as a female form appears at an upper window, framed in flame, curtained with smoke and noxious fumes.

'Save her! Save her', yells the crowd.

The crowd sways and surges, women scream, strong men clench their hands and swear – heaven only knows why. But before the police have headed back the people, the escape is on the spot, two men are on it, one outstrips his mate, and darting up the ladder, leaps into the open window.

He is swallowed up in a moment – lost to our sight. Will he ever return out of that fiery furnace? Yes, here he is, bearing a senseless female form, which

Opposite: The fire engine leaving the West Norwood station, c1890.
(London Metropolitan Archives, SC/PHL/CL/04/01/045)

he passes out to his mate, who is calmly watching his progress, though the ladder is in imminent danger. Quick! The flames approach!

The man on the ladder does not wait as his mate again disappears and emerges with a child of about fourteen. Carrying this burden easily, he descends the ladder. The first man is already flying down the escape, headfirst, holding the woman's dress around her feet. The others, rescuer and rescued, follow. The ladder is withdrawn, burning.

A mighty cheer arises amid the smoke. Two lives saved! The fire is being mastered. More engines gallop up. The captain is on the spot, too. The Brigade is victorious."

This account, taken from the *Strand Magazine* in the 1890s, evokes the true drama and bravery of those firefighters of the period when West Norwood Fire Station was operating at its peak, based at the fire station on Norwood High Street.

FIREFIGHTING IN THE 19TH CENTURY

In the early 1800s, fires were fought with a combination of volunteers and brigades that were funded by insurance companies. As profit-making businesses, the focus of these insurance firms was

on saving properties rather than lives, and the lack of co-ordination and rivalry between the insurance-funded brigades was regularly criticised [Butti, December 2013].

Parish vestries, the precursors to municipal authorities and borough councils, were obliged to keep and maintain engines for pumping water and providing access to public water supplies in the event of a fire. They were not, however, obliged to provide a fire crew, although some parishes did.

In 1832 The London Fire Engine Establishment was formed by the insurance companies and increasingly it was called upon to deal with fires to uninsured property, most famously the Houses of Parliament in

Above: Sir Eyre Massey Shaw, the first Superintendent of the London Fire Brigade. (London Fire Brigade Museum)

1863. Unwilling to be responsible for London's fire protection due to escalating compensation costs, the insurance companies put pressure on the government. This led to an act of Parliament, passed in 1865, which enabled the formation of the Metropolitan Fire Brigade.

THE METROPOLITAN FIRE BRIGADE

Formed in 1866, the Metropolitan Police Service was initially responsible for controlling the Metropolitan Fire Brigade (MFB), but this authority was soon passed to the Metropolitan Board of Works (MBW), and in 1904 it was renamed the London Fire Brigade.

Captain Sir Eyre Massey Shaw was appointed Chief Officer of the MFB and set about changing

it significantly. He established a new rank system, and decided to recruit exclusively from the Navy, as sailors had already learnt discipline and were used to working both day and night. Firemen at that time were on call permanently and had very little leave. He also introduced a new uniform that consisted of a brass helmet, a navy-blue woollen tunic, cloth trousers, leather boots, belt with pouch and an axe.

Above left: The strong, distinctive brass helmet had front and back peaks to protect the head, with an ear section cut away to enable the firemen to hear. (London Fire Brigade Museum)

Above right: Cadbury's advert. (Cadbury Archive, Mondelēz International)

Captain Shaw also built new fire stations, and introduced the most advanced technology of the day to improve the service. He brought in steam fire engines that could pump, on average, 300 gallons of water a minute.

> "Horses were used to pull the engines and they were housed at the station with the firefighters. Sloping floors in fire stations allowed engines to move out more easily – this was called 'on the run', a term still used today.
>
> At the time of the creation of the Metropolitan Fire Brigade, the government realised that there were inadequate resources to fight fires in the rapidly growing city. A plan was drawn up for the creation of an additional 24 Fire Brigade stations, including the one at West Norwood.
> ~ *Jackson, W.E., 1966*

THE FIRST WEST NORWOOD FIRE STATION

At this time the nearest fire station to serve West Norwood was on Crystal Palace Parade in Upper Norwood, but the land to the south-east of St Luke's Church became available, and West Norwood Fire Station was the first building to be constructed there, with work starting in 1881. Norwood High Street was chosen for the site because it was the highest point of Lower Norwood, as the area had previously been called, giving the horse-drawn appliances the advantage of going downhill to most locations, so being able to reach them more quickly.

Built and designed by the Metropolitan Board of Works and its architect Robert Pearsall, the building's style is Gothic, sometimes called Victorian Gothic, and the MBW sign can still be seen above the front doors, near the date of 1881.

West Norwood Fire Station is the only remaining Victorian fire station for horse-drawn tenders in England, with the two historical features of the original red fire doors and the octagonal lookout tower still in place. It is Grade II-listed and designated as a building of national historical interest by English Heritage.

Comprising three main storeys with attics, the building is composed of red brick in English Bond, with a tiled roof. The attic storey has four gables, four chimney stacks and timber sash windows and takes in two paired eight-pane windows at each end and two single 12-paned windows in the centre. A creamy-white Portland stone band below the

Opposite: Postcard sent in 1881, looking south-east across St Luke's Church, with Crystal Palace beyond. (Lambeth Archives Department, www.landmark.lambeth.gov.uk ref 4626)

windows is supported by 16 brick-and-stone corbels, acting as brackets.

The first and second floors both have eight 8-paned sash windows, while the first-floor windows have arched lintels interrupting a moulded terracotta band, a favoured architectural design of the time.

Eight 8-paned windows are also found on the ground floor, under a drip moulding on either side of the central projecting porch with gable surmounted by central and side finials. Below this porch are the two wide fire doors, each framed with a pair of decorative red colonnettes. The full width of these doors was used for the horse-drawn fire appliances to leave when attending a fire, and the fire station sign was mounted centrally above.

The principal feature of the fire station is the

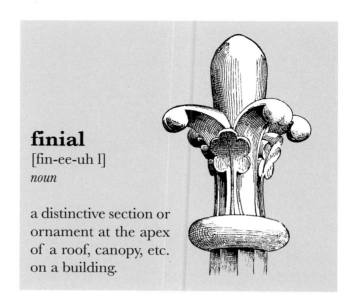

finial
[fin-ee-uh l]
noun

a distinctive section or ornament at the apex of a roof, canopy, etc. on a building.

distinctive, tall, octagonal watch tower at the northern end, featuring corbelling and lancet (or slit) windows, and another terracotta band. From the top of the tower, firemen could spot the location of fires and, importantly, they could hang the canvas hoses inside the tower to dry out after use, preventing deterioration from mould growth.

According to JB Wilson, a local funeral director and amateur photographer, the result of the university boat race on the Thames was signalled from the flag

English Bond brickwork is found most often in older houses and buildings. The wall's thickness is the length of the brick.

Within each row the bricks are laid in the same direction. Different variations of this bonding may be used.

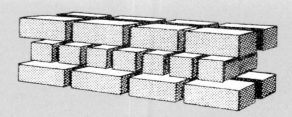

An example of English Bond brickwork.

mast at the top of the tower by hoisting either a light-blue or dark-blue flag.

To the left of the building the horses returned through the gates via a side "run-in", back into the yard, enabling the horses to lead the appliances into the area behind the doors, so that they were facing forward and ready for the next call.

The rear elevation has square lintels over its 12 sash windows, instead of the arched Gothic lintels at the front, with moulded terracotta bands between the cream Portland stone bands over the windows. The MBW sign can be seen near the ribbed chimneys. A blue London County Council (LCC) sign was added later, probably sometime between 1900 and 1910.

EVERYDAY LIFE AT THE FIRE STATION

Operational from 1882 until 1916, the station's firemen attended many incidents that were reported in both local and national newspapers. Calls for rescue came to the station in several ways: sometimes people ran to the station door, and other times a system of "street alarms" were placed at strategic locations throughout the station's area.

Previous: A horse-drawn escape exits the building via the central doors, after 1897. Postcard image.

This alarm system was established in 1890 by the Lambeth Board of Guardians, which realised the need to protect the safety of parish schools. The fitting for the telegraph wires from the street alarms is evident at the watch tower's north-west corner.

BOGUS FIRE BRIGADE IN WEST NORWOOD

Three local firemen were brought before the Common Serjeant in 1892 and charged with conspiracy to cheat and defraud. It was alleged that they had promoted the "West Norwood Fire Escape Brigade", which was shown to be a sham, but during the previous 12 months the accused had raised funds amounting to £70, more than £60,000 at today's value, by public subscription. All three were committed for trial at the Central Criminal Court, where a number of tradespeople testified that they had been approached by the accused and pressed to donate money for a new fire station.

As their defence, the accused claimed that they were in possession of a dilapidated fire-escape [a

Opposite: This early photograph of the fire station shows the gates at the southern end of the building where the returning horse-drawn appliances would enter the premises. The flag mast on the tower can be seen and one of the main doors remains open, possibly while the firemen were out on call, 1906. (LMA SC/PHL/02/482/3578)

A horse-drawn "steamer" of the type used by the West Norwood Brigade. c1900 (LMA)

TELEGRAPH ALARM

The street fire-alarm system was used to summon the West Norwood Brigade to a serious fire at Albert Cottages, West Norwood, in 1887. The fire had broken out on the first floor of Mr Rendall's residence. When the firemen arrived, the first and second floors were ablaze and the fire extended to the building next door before it could be brought under control by the use of a 'plentiful supply of water'.

~ Croydon Advertiser
& East Surrey Reporter, 1887

On 17 May, the West Norwood Brigade attended a bridge [fire] on the London, Brighton and South Coast Railway thought to have been triggered by a spark from a steam locomotive, an ever-present danger in the days of steam power.

~ Nottingham Evening Post, 1887

In July, in spite of three brigades, including West Norwood and Crystal Palace, attending a fire at Borrowdale, a house in Lawrie Park Gardens, the prompt action of PC Aycliff and residents had the conflagration under control using pails of water!

~ Croydon Advertiser
& East Surrey Reporter, 1891

horse-drawn fire appliance with an escape ladder mounted on it] which was housed on wasteland on Knight's Hill. The Chief Fire Officer of the West Norwood station, Edward Day, gave evidence stating that "in the six years he had worked there he had never seen the fire-escape attend a fire."

The three were found guilty and sentenced to four months' imprisonment, without hard labour.

'STEAMER' TO THE RESCUE

" The failure, sometimes, by the brigade to successfully deal with fires is illustrated by the total destruction of Mr Bennett's furniture depository in 1892, a mere five-minute walk along Norwood Road from the fire station!

~ London Evening Standard, 1892

Firefighting was a hazardous occupation with occasionally serious consequences. John Nicholas, of the West Norwood Brigade, suffered a serious accident while attending a fire at 165 Tulse Hill, less than three-quarters of a mile from the station. Fireman Nicholas, while attempting to extinguish it, fell through a window and into the building. He attempted to fight on but was carried away by his colleagues, and later a doctor found him to have a fractured rib and injuries to the head. Fortunately, he made a full recovery.

As it is now, the West Norwood Brigade was called out at all times of the day and night, and provided the service 365 days of the year. It was also home to the West Norwood 'Steamer', a horse-drawn steam engine and pump.

Metropolitan Board of Works chief engineer, Joseph Bazalgette, most famous for planning London's sewer network in the 1850s, reported in 1877 to a select committee that 'jets for extinguishing fires could not be obtained by the waterworks pressure in the metropolis, and that the pumping power of the jets must be supplied by the fire engines.'
~ *Building News and Engineering Journal, 1877*

The West Norwood steam-powered pump was called in to help to extinguish a fire at Westow Hill in Upper Norwood on 21 December, 1898. Williamsons Ltd's premises at number 14 was alight, probably the result of ashes from a boiler setting fire to nearby woodwork. However, by the time the 'steamer' arrived, all danger was over, thanks to the Crystal Palace and Croydon brigades.
~ *Croydon Advertiser & East Surrey Reporter, 1898*

In April 1898 another fire in a boiler room brought both West Norwood and Sydenham brigades to attend the scene at a nursery on Westow Hill. The contents of the building and many plants stored there were severely damaged before the fire was brought under control.
~ *London Daily News, 1898*

The value of the 'steamer' was again evident when it came to the rescue when dealing with a serious blaze involving five houses in Church Road, Upper Norwood. The Crystal Palace and Thornton Heath brigades had failed to obtain sufficient pressure from the nearby hydrants and the houses were enveloped in flames of great strength. The situation became even more desperate as the fire spread to adjoining buildings and the cry went up that there were

Above: Children gather outside their school building on Elder Road, behind a call point on the street, after an incident of fire. c1890 (LAD)

*The West Norwood 'Steamer' attending a fire on Auckland Hill in 1914.
On the left the manual escape is wheeled into position. (LAD)*

persons still sleeping in the houses. Local firemen E Austell and J Morris entered the inferno at great risk to themselves and, to the cheers of the crowd, rescued two women – Mrs Sarlow and Mrs Hall – who had been asleep when the fire broke out.

Fanned by a brisk wind, the flames burst through the roof and quickly spread to adjoining properties. Fortunately, the day was saved, if not the buildings, by the arrival of the West Norwood 'Steamer', which used its on-board steam pump to propel two jets of water high into the air, right over the three-storey building, and bring the raging fire under control.

~ Croydon Advertiser & East Surrey Reporter, 1899

A paraffin lamp of the type that killed Mrs Whiteman. (Image Courtesy of The Canterbury Auction Galleries)

INQUESTS

Firemen were not only called upon to fight fires, but also to attend inquests to offer their experience and knowledge in attempting to understand the cause of fires and to suggest ways of avoiding them. Thus, the Chief Fire Officer of the West Norwood Brigade, Stephen Richards, was present at the inquest of Mrs Julia Whiteman of Brixton Hill in 1900. She had dropped a lit paraffin lamp and set fire to her clothing in the bedroom of her house. Chief Officer Richards described finding the smashed china reservoir on the bedroom floor when he attended the scene. A verdict of accidental death was recorded.

~ London Daily News, 1900

Suffragettes Annie Kenny and Christabel Pankhurst, 1906. (National Archives COPY 01/494/1906)

SUFFRAGETTES

Action by the suffragettes brought the West Norwood, Dulwich Park and Herne Hill brigades into action on the night of 5 September 1913. As part of their campaign for women's suffrage, they set fire to laboratories in two wings of Dulwich College. After the fires were extinguished, suffragette literature was found pinned to trees in the college grounds. Students were away on holiday and, although there was damage, there was no loss of life.

~ *Yorkshire and Leeds Intelligencer, 1913*

OPERATIONAL LIFE

The operational centre of the fire station was the watch room, situated next to the appliance bay, behind the central doors. There was always someone on duty there, often the superintendent, and all firemen and their families had to report their whereabouts and observe a strict curfew. This room also acted as a place for firemen to rest while waiting to be called out, and as the area for keeping the kit of the men on watch, so that they could change quickly. A full uniform kit room was upstairs, probably next to the dormitories, while the firemen's trunks were kept in the basement.

Fire appliances themselves were horse-drawn, although the horses were not owned by the Brigade, but leased, at considerable expense, from one of several companies that provided horses across London. For example, in 1915, the cost of leasing a horse and its equipment for a year was almost as much as the wages of a middle-ranking fireman – £70, compared with £92. One of the firms supplying horses was Thomas Tilling Ltd, which had stables next to the Paxton Tavern on the road to the Crystal Palace. He provided horses for coaches going to the Palace and may well have supplied them to West Norwood Fire Station. Horses used for this work had to be sufficiently strong to pull the heavy 'Steamer' without breaking into a gallop.

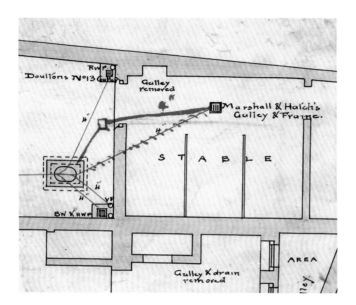

Stabling was situated on site, but space was limited and the plan of 1896 shows only three stalls. Room was also needed for storing the horses' tack, straw for bedding and food. This yard served many purposes, including as storage for coal, as a workshop for repairing equipment, and as a washdown area for horses and appliances, as well as an area for drill practice. Coachmen would also have lived on the ground floor, or under the first floor, in order to be near the horses.

The typical head coachman in the Brigade was paid 40s 6d a week, with free quarters, coal and light supplied, after 15 years of service.

By 1908 the fire station housed a station officer, nine foremen, two coachmen, two pairs of horses, one

*Above: Stables shown on Holloway's 1869 drainage plan.
(Lambeth Archives Department)*

steam fire engine, one horse-drawn escape, one manual escape and a horse cart. Manual escapes were large, wooden extension ladders mounted on a carriage that could be pushed to the scene of a fire and were incredibly stable. Sometimes they were left tied to lamp-posts for use in an emergency, and were stationed around the streets with attendant 'escape conductors' to man them.

FIREMEN AND THEIR FAMILIES

At the end of the 19th century, life was not easy for many, but for the firemen and their families, things could have been much worse, as they were required to live in accommodation that was provided by the Brigade. In West Norwood, however, because of the lack of space in the station, in 1901 at least six families were based in small two-up-two-down houses in nearby Dunbar Street.

This arrangement of men living off-site made for some difficulties in running the station. The firemen were not always close to hand, though when on duty they were probably based within the station.

The 1901 census shows that six employees were housed in the main station, along with their families,

Opposite: East Place, West Norwood, c1900. (LAD)

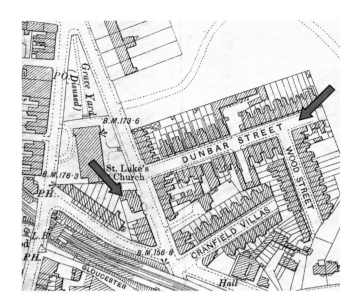

six in Dunbar Street, and one more on nearby Auckland Hill. The station officer was Stephen Thomas Richards, senior both in rank and age, who had the luxury of his own flat on the top floor of the station building, where he lived along with his wife and six children.

The other firemen and coachmen lived on the first and second floors, all with their own rooms but probably sharing facilities such as kitchens and bathrooms. A total of 14 children lived at the station, and only two of the firemen were unmarried. George Thresher was the only one among them who appears to have been at the station for very long and he was allocated the Auckland Hill accommodation.

Frederick Nile was a typical fireman of the time, having served in at least eight stations during his career. Born in north London, he moved around assignments in Islington, Finsbury, Homerton, Hampstead and Enfield, as well as his stint in West Norwood. He also lived to a good age, dying in Hampstead in 1956.

Coachman/groom William Parmenter moved to West Norwood from the Shadwell station, where he was based in 1891. He died in Walthamstow aged 69.

Coachman Charles Botley seems to have travelled further than any of the other firemen, for he was born in Sydney, Australia, in 1872. Records show that by 1911 he was stationed at Shoreditch, and he died in Hastings, East Sussex, in 1957, aged 86.

George Thresher, born in Shenley in Hertfordshire, came from a different background. He had been an able seaman on HMS *Martin*, which was a 16-gun brig, launched in 1850, then used for training from 1890 and renamed HMS *Kingfisher*.

The census of 1901 suggests that, despite doing an arduous and sometimes dangerous job, the firemen seem to have lived on into retirement, often reaching ages well in excess of those that might be expected for the general population.

Above: Ordnance Survey map of 1894 showing the cottages in Dunbar Street. Described as 'some 70 yards from the station' the firemen would have been in the conventional houses at the far end of the street (since demolished) rather than the model cottages/maisonettes which survive. (Ordnance Survey Godfrey Edition)

Above: Surviving Dunbar St cottages 1-11. Front and side entrances for the four families that occupied each block. (Stephen Oxford, 2017)

The six cottages numbered 7 to 17 were occupied by firemen stationed at West Norwood Fire Station in both the 1901 and 1911 censuses. Although small, the living conditions in the cottages were probably better than those in the fire station, and in 1901, 19

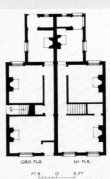

people were living there. During the Blitz of the Second World War, a large high-explosive bomb fell on Dunbar Street and demolished a great swathe of these houses.

Left: Floor plan of 25-29 Dunbar Street. (English Heritage Archive)

DUNBAR STREET

Land companies and building societies built houses for their members, and were active in West Norwood in the second half of the 19th century. The Lower Norwood Co-operative Building Company erected humble, working-class cottages on the Elm Grove Estate on Dunbar Street. The first of these were built in 1865 and each pair contained four lettings with separate entrances.

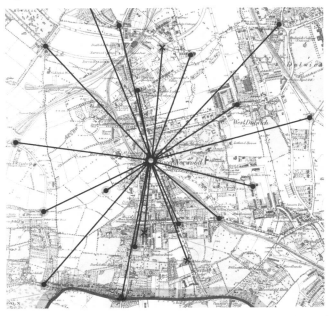

Above: Facsimile of a Call Point map from 1907 showing West Norwood Station at the centre and the call points in the surrounding area which connected to it. (Version Bryon Fear 2018)

MOVING ON

In the early years of the 20th century, West Norwood Fire Station was rapidly becoming unsatisfactory and was deemed no longer 'fit for purpose'. Developments in technology meant that its accommodation for equipment was very restricted, and the main doors were not able to cope with the newer appliances. Accommodation for firemen and their families, even supplemented by the housing in Dunbar Street, was cramped and unsuitable.

By 1908 things were coming to a head and, in his report to the Fire Brigade Committee of December that year, the chief officer, James de Courcy Hamilton, wrote:

" Doubtless the Committee will know that the congested nature of the station is such that the poles have to be removed from the appliances before the horses can be placed in position. Further, on several occasions damage has been done to the station in turning out with the horse escape. The recreation room is very small and not sufficiently large for duty men to sleep in any degree of comfort.

The search began for a site on which to build a larger replacement station. Several locations were considered by the committee over the next few

years, including the possibility of St Luke's Church. Some ideas fell through as land was sold to other purchasers, and some proved unsuitable. A proposal to extend the existing station was considered, but it soon became clear from the plans that this would be far from satisfactory. It could provide a third appliance bay and seven more rooms, but this still would not result in sufficient accommodation.

After considerable delays and changes of plans, a plot was acquired and a new station built at 445 Norwood Road. Construction took place during the First World War, a time when building works were generally frozen by the Metropolitan Fire Brigade. Notices that a new fire station was to be built for West Norwood appeared in several newspapers, quoting the sum of £13,777 for its construction.
~ *Surrey Mirror, 1914*

It opened in 1916 and the station officer and firemen were transferred to much improved quarters there.

Above: The Norwood Road Fire Station which was built in 1916.
(© London Fire Brigade, Mary Evans Picture Library)

ST LUKE'S CHURCH

Fortunately for the old building, the original station's neighbour was St Luke's Church, which had been searching for land on which to build accommodation to house its many social and spiritual activities.

The need for more suitable premises was drawn to parishioners' attention by the vicar in 1914. He stated that a parish hall was an absolute necessity to the parish and he wondered how work had gone on for so long without one. A proposal was considered to build on the east side of the church yard, just north of the fire station, but this was consecrated ground and there was reluctance to use it for secular purposes. The problem of finding freehold land that the church could afford proved insurmountable at that time and little was achieved over the next few years, particularly with the outbreak of war in 1914.

Once the decision had been made to build a new fire station, disposal of the old one had to be considered and the Valuer was instructed to look for a purchaser. Thus, two needs coincided and St Luke's raised sufficient funds to purchase the building and convert it to serve as its parish hall. The first parish meeting of 1917 was held there and an appeal to raise £500 to carry out the necessary alterations was discussed.
~ *Quoted by Butti, December 2013*

By March of that year permission had been granted to go ahead with the necessary alterations, but due to the shortage of suitable labour at a time when the country was still at war, none were carried out. The church continued to raise money, with the vicar announcing that the sum of £93 0s 6d had been promised even before the appeal was made public.
~ *Quoted by Butti, December 2013*

Alterations did eventually proceed and great use of the old fire station was made by St Luke's for nearly 50 years. However, by the early 1960s, the vicar of the time was greatly lamenting its purchase and use as a parish hall.

Above: St Luke's Parish Church, W Norwood, 1937.
(Illustration by FR Hardcastle, St Luke's Archive)

CHAPTER TWO

The fire station lives on as St Luke's parish hall 1917-47

When St Luke's Church purchased the fire station on 24 July 1917 from the London County Council, only fairly minor alterations were made at first, and it was not fully adapted for church purposes for almost a decade. However, it did give much-needed space for the myriad activities and services that the church provided for the community, and was a valuable addition to the church's facilities.

There was something going on at St Luke's every day of the week. The 1917 Parish Magazine lists a whole host of meetings held in its various spaces:

Choir practice; mothers' meetings; Sunday school teachers; British Red Cross; Girls' Friendly Society; Lads' Club; district visitors; Communicants' Guild; Finance Committee; Church Council; Band of Hope; Missionary Club; Mens' Club; Church Bible Study Union; Mothers' Union; Coal and Clothing Club; Penny Bank; Sick Club; National Schools; Mission Church; Boys' Club; and many other church societies.

District visitors were the volunteer precursors of social workers, visiting people in their homes, while the Coal Club and Penny Bank were schemes to help working-class people save. The Girls' Friendly Society sought to keep young women out of trouble and to improve their opportunities by pairing disadvantaged girls with young women of a "better class" from the church and arranging social and educational activities. The St Luke's Girls' Club met every Friday for a subscription of 1d a week, with occasional dances as a highlight.

The 1917 Parish Magazine also strikes a sombre note, with much mention of the war. It contains no reference to the purchase of the fire station, but it could be that some may have thought it wrong to make such an outlay on property when no one knew what the future might bring.

The verger in 1917 was Mr W J Thorn, but by 1919

Opposite: Norwood High Street from St Luke's Church, c1905. (LAD)

the acting verger, Mr Scarff, occupied the top floor of the fire station and was paid a monthly wage of £2 10s, with extra payments for cleaning duties. He also acted as the caretaker and took on whatever repairs were needed.

In May 1917 it was decided that nurses could also be accommodated in the new parish hall, on the second floor, and were housed there until 1924. In June 1917 the Nurses' Committee asked for the nurses' cupboard to be brought down to the ground floor in case of air raids to store messages securely for the staff.

Social activities were given a boost in July 1917 with the formation of a card room next to the billiard room, down in the basement – for the men only, at that time. The social club was open every weekday and on Saturdays. St Luke's took its social responsibilities seriously, with the intention of keeping men entertained without recourse to drinking or gambling, apart from the permitted Sunday card games – football matches were planned for the same reason.

The new parish hall was officially opened by Sir William Samuel on 4 April 1918.

There were plans to extend the new hall at the fire station, but financial difficulties repeatedly delayed

these. In November 1919, outgoings were £140 while income was £70 – a parlous state of affairs. Despite these problems, in 1918 it was decided to try to buy the piece of land between the church and fire station for a sum not exceeding £200. It took some time to raise the money, but the deal was completed by December that year.

In the coming years, Four Day Bazaars were held annually as very successful fundraisers, with more than £1,000 added to the coffers several years in succession, gradually providing enough funds to make the major alterations needed.

Eventually, in 1927, architectural plans were drawn up by Ernest G Cole, of 12 Bedford Row, the work was tendered and a contract for £3,580 awarded to Messrs Dix and Co, builders. The final cost, however, was £5,550 excluding fees, furnishing and fittings. A single-storey extension was attached to the southern side of the fire station, with additional single-storey extensions to the north and to the

Above: Group of Voluntary Aid Detachments nurses, c1914-1918.
(British Red Cross Archive, IN4467)

rear in the west. Although little is known about Mr Cole, all the work was executed with carefully matched materials.

Another major addition was an ornate, spiral, cast-iron fire escape staircase attached to the rear of the building, reaching up to the top floor, with windows converted to doors on two floors, giving access to the staircase.

Once work had commenced in June 1927, the vicar laid a commemorative stone to mark the extension in August, and the hall, even though it was not quite finished, was opened by Lady Greaves-Lord on 30 November of that year.

Above: The spiral staircase at the rear of the building, 2015 (Bryon Fear)

ALTERATIONS OF 1927

The building work required was extensive and provided additional parish halls and rooms tailored to the church's needs. Major alterations were made to strengthen some areas of the building with a new structure of steel stanchions and beams supporting the upper floors and a large asphalted roof. Throughout the work, every effort was made to match up external as well as internal fixtures such as plaster moulding and skirting boards. New doors were added with others blocked up, as the interior and exterior was rebuilt and reorganised.

Third floor
The top-floor rooms have been in continuous use as accommodation throughout the history of the building. Having more stairs to climb and with rooms decorated more cheaply, it was initially the junior firemen who were housed there, but then vergers from St Luke's Church also used this accommodation, as did parish caretakers after 1927.

Second floor
Two rooms on the second floor were used as nurses' and caretaker's accommodation before 1927, but then the Social Club moved out of the basement into these rooms, meaning that the billiard table had to be taken down each week to accommodate the Sunday School.

First floor
The largest room on this floor had been divided into two rooms as married quarters for the firemen, each containing a fireplace, an iron grate and a mantlepiece. St Luke's removed these partitions.

Labels on the shelves show that these rooms were used to store choir music, and the cupboards and hooks held the choir robes. Immediately after the 1927 refurbishment, two of the choir boys managed to break the window glass, and their letters of apology featured in the parish magazine (see box). One of the windows in this room was also converted into French doors that led out to the new flat roof.

SPOKEN LIKE GENTLEMEN – HOW TO MEND BROKEN GLASS

A room in the beautiful new hall had been fitted with wardrobe-cupboards for choirboys' use, and had been given to them as a Sunday vestry. Unfortunately the room also contained a window. Released from the constraint of the series of Sunday services culminating in Evensong, the small choristers managed to break a window. Nobody knew who had done it! The result was a castigation from the Vicar, coupled with the dire warning that the lovely new vestry would be taken away from them. But by the following Wednesday, after an interview with their choirmaster, two small boys came to

Dear Sir,—I must apoligize for breaking that window on Sunday night, as it was an accident. I am willingly going to do my best to help to pay for it. Although I am a new member to your choir I hope I will not do such a thing again. I must close being,—Yours sincerely, Member of St. Luk's Choir.

Dear Sir,—I am writing to opologise for breaking the window on Sunday evening last. It happened when —— and I put our heads through it, and —— and I promised to pay for it.—I remain your faithful servant,

——

see the vicar and handed him the letters printed above (names have been omitted). Most readers will agree that an "accident" like this could happen to anybody, and that by "apologising" in such a brave, true fashion and offering to pay for the damage the Church choirboys brought credit to themselves, their Choirmaster and to the Church they belonged.

Above: St Luke's Church News – March 1928. (St Luke's Archive)

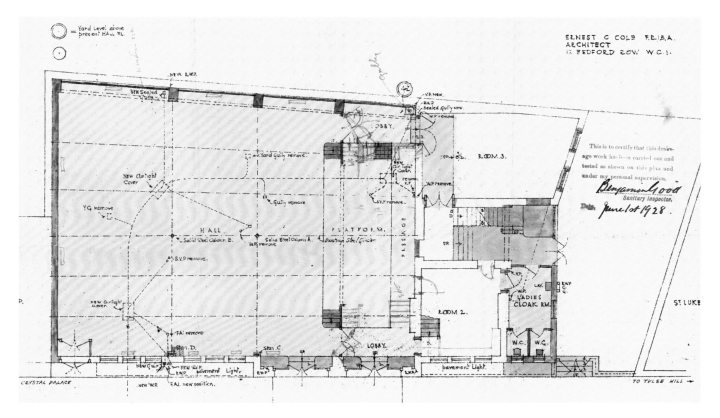

The first, second and third floors all feature a corridor facing south, from which all the rooms opened, while one window on each corridor was changed to a door in order to give access to the imposing cast-iron fire escape staircase.

Ground floor
During the refurbishment, the ground floor was extended over the whole plot to the south, with additions to the north (between the church and fire station), and to the west (at the rear). The south and west walls of the appliance bay were removed to form the main new parish hall, while extra doors to the street were also added. An exterior plaque records the 1927 extension.

The original floor of the appliance bay was of ironstone or cobbles, to prevent the horses slipping, and sloped down slightly to the street. Having seen plenty of use by both horses and fire appliances, St Luke's needed to take up the floor when it took over. Woodblock finish, or parquet, was laid, and while the bay doors remained, timber lobbies were introduced for acoustic and draught protection.

When the new parish room was extended, the original yard was enclosed, together with the appliance bay, making a much larger space for the parish hall.

Above: E Cole's extension plans for St Luke's, 1927. (LAD)

Presciently, a stage area was created at the north end of the room and performances took place here, long before the building became a theatre in 1967. Although a passage behind the stage was intended, plans were changed and a flight of stairs led to the watch room instead.

The floor levels have been changed many times over the years. In the 1927 refurbishment, the area to the north became a dual-purpose area, at times a foyer to the main hall and at others an additional parish room, if the large hall was in use. Double doors connected it to the new side entrance.

Basement floor

A staircase was inserted so that the kitchen could directly serve the main hall above, which led up to the site of the original watch room. The wash house on this floor became the kitchen and its stone-flagged floor remained until 2015.

Above the sink in the kitchen, pavement lights added illumination to the basement. Often called "illuminating vault covers", these lights were examples of the Thaddeus Hyatt prism system, originally invented in the US. These were possibly inserted pre-1927 as there were originally railings set forward in front of this part of the building.

Small, thick glass discs, or lenses, were set into iron

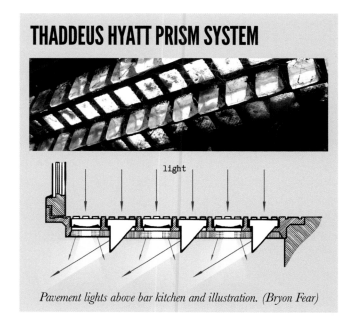

THADDEUS HYATT PRISM SYSTEM

Pavement lights above bar kitchen and illustration. (Bryon Fear)

covers in such a way that the glass was protected from damage. However, prisms attached to the underside of the lenses admitted reflected and refracted light into the basement, while letting in natural light and "avoiding the need for gas lighting and its attendant fumes," in a confined space.
~ *Historic Prism Glass Companies of the United States*
T Hyatt

The social club in the basement was well attended, and one area had been used as a card room. Though not shown on the 1927 plan, ironmongery suggests that a fire escape was installed at this time, leading from the back of the bar to ground level.

In the January 1928 newsletter, the vicar noted that "we are promised the hall by Christmas week". However, as the New Hall Committee was still making decisions about some items that the architect needed to finish on 12 December, this was optimistic.

MISS L F NOTT

Miss Nott has somehow found time to read for and pass the inter-diocesan examinations in theology and pastoralia.

These successes entitle her to official "recognition" by the bishop as an approved "Woman Worker" in the church.

St Luke's Church News – October 1928
(LMA P85/LUK/110)

A decision was made to appoint a resident caretaker, to live in the rooms then occupied by a Mr Brown, and be responsible for general care and cleaning, including locking up at night. Mr Brown would be found suitable accommodation elsewhere and revert to the position of verger only.

The Bishop of Woolwich dedicated the hall on 13 February 1928, with much publicity, but decisions were still being made about the fitting out of the hall in March for costs not included in the original estimate, with a payment being deferred in July.

The debt on the hall, which took the form of a £3,000 loan from Barclays Bank and a £1,000 interest-free loan from the diocese, was steadily reduced, and by 1933 was less than £1,000.

THEATRICAL INCLINATIONS

The building's theatrical leanings had started even before the opening, with a performance of JM Barrie's *Dear Brutus* by the Norwood Players, that contributed to the parish hall funds. A performance in the new hall of *Tilly of Bloomsbury* by Ian Hay on 9 February in aid of the Sunday School was closely followed on 17 February by the parish's Young Persons Service Dramatic Society production of *Scenes from Pickwick*. The Norwood Players boasted that its cast included local celebrities such as the Misses Florence and Dorothea Shugar and Mr William Harris (instructor in elocution at the Technical Institute).

Bazaars and theatre performances continued to be a great success. The bazaar of 1928 advertised "Orchestras, Wireless, Entertainments, Competitions and 25 stalls" and was open from 3pm to 10pm each day.

As the years passed the hall continued to serve the community with a wide range of activities and services, while adapting to the ever-changing needs of the times. For instance, during the 1930s and 1940s BBC radio services were transmitted from, or at least recorded in, the hall.

CHAPTER THREE

The decline and sale of St Luke's parish hall 1947-67

For many years the fire station building was used as a church hall, providing space for community activities intended to engage people, young and old, in the life of the church; to raise funds; to provide moral and social education, to contribute to spiritual and intellectual development; as well as providing entertainment for the local community. During the 1935 election it was also used as a local counting office.

The accounts for the church hall for 1946 mark the beginning of the decline in income. During the 1950s, although the hall continued to be used regularly by a wide range of groups, income fell steadily and was often outstripped by expenditure.

In a parish newsletter from the 1950s, the vicar stated that activities in the church hall occurred from Monday morning until Saturday night.

During this decade there grew a tradition of performances in the hall, often by the Girl Guides or the local youth club, but also by the Norman Players, which put on productions of *Charlie's Aunt*, *Wishing Well*, *The Happiest Days of Your Life*, *Fit for Heroes*, *But Once a Year* and *Without the Prince*. The Norman Players' shows were produced by Norman Freeman, who sometimes appeared in minor roles, and they regularly received glowing reviews.

During the 1950s and 1960s, there were regular activities in the hall, including church AGMs, Christmas and New Year parties, jumble sales and bazaars, youth clubs, working party sales, Girl Guides, Brownies, Cubs, Scouts, sewing parties, concerts, Sunday School, whist drives and Christmas fayres.

Many local groups also made use of the hall, such as The King's Messengers, social committees, the

Opposite: Old Folks Tea at St Luke's Church hall. Visit of the Mayor Alderman W Lockyer, and Mayoress, 28 March 1945. (LAD www.landmark.lambeth.gov.uk ref 324)

Young Wives' Club, Woman's Hour, Young Communicants, the Mothers' Union, the Lads' Club, the Old Scholars Club and the Clothing Club.

During the mid-1950s activities began to diminish as other forms of entertainment such as television became more widely available. The Mothers' Union and Woman's Hour were still going strong, however, and were reported in detail in the parish magazine.

Things were even worse by the late 1950s, with attendances at events falling off drastically. In 1958 film shows were given to attract greater attendance at Woman's Hour. Bazaars and jumble sales were smaller and less frequent, generally raising minimal sums towards running costs.

During 1960, in an effort to save money, the youth group, to the consternation of the vicar, redecorated some of the church hall, when it was being used for worship in 1962 while the church was redecorated and war damage repaired.

In the magazine of October 1960 the vicar of St Luke's Church wrote, in some desperation, an account of the use of the building by the church.

"It began, of course, as a fire station, all five floors, including the little red tower from which the hoses were suspended to dry them after use.

Unfortunately, St Luke's bought it and spent more on its adaptation than would have been needed to build a modern church hall. It has been a white elephant ever since, requiring to be let to the outside public for all kinds of purposes in order to provide enough money to meet its heavy overheads. But this is a vicious circle, for the more it is let the more it costs to run it and the greater the need for repairs.

He included societal changes as part of the problem.

"In recent years things have got much worse, for two reasons. First, television has brought about a … revolution in people's habits. Those who once went out for amusement now stay at home. There is much to be said for this … in its reinstatement of the home and family as the centre of life. But all who have catered in the past for outside enjoyment have suffered as a result, and the church has had strange bedfellows, for it has been affected equally with the cinema, the dance and public house. People today … often do not want outside weekday activities and the church finds it difficult to provide socials … for its people. So the demand for letting in regard to St

Above: Rev Dr Francis J Lambert. (St Luke's Church Archive)

CHURCH HALL

EXPENDITURE.	£	s.	d.
Wages and National Insurance ...	186	11	4
Licences	5	4	0
Repairs and Renewals	291	7	4
Refunds to Missions, etc.	5	5	0
Laundry, Postage and Sundries ...	24	19	10
Fuel, Light and Cleaning	107	12	10
Rates	46	5	10
Fire and Burglary Insurance	8	6	3
Fees	23	1	8
	698	14	1
Cash in hand (Hall Secretary), 31st December, 1947 ...	31	12	0
Balance in hand (Treasurer), 31st December, 1947 (a)	903	1	0
	£1.633	7	1

(a) Against this balance there is a liability of £776 12s. 6d. for repairs.

INCOME.	£	s.	d.
Hall Lettings	644	3	4
War Damage Commission	35	12	0
Ministry of Works Compensation ...	399	14	6
	1.079	9	10
Cash with Hall Secretary, 1st January, 1947	18	13	8
Balance in hand, 1st January, 1947 ...	535	3	7
	£1.633	7	1

Luke's Hall has changed out of all knowledge in the past 10 years. Second, the labour situation has changed, and it is a very difficult matter getting a hall-keeper to live in a flat four floors up and do endless work of maintaining a hall in such constant use.

He described his attempts to tackle these issues:

" My first solution was to combine the positions of hall-keeper, verger and parish clerk, with commensurate increase in wages and a much more interesting job of work to be done. We provided a verger's office in the hall, with a telephone, and it worked very well for the five years Mr Haynes filled the position.

Selling the hall was discussed with the local authority.

" Since then the problems have become worse, with less letting for more outlay and increasing deterioration. If we could have sold it we would have done so, but we are governed by town planning regulations. Finally, we had an offer by a commercial firm to take over the ground and lower floors at a very substantial rent. We requested planning permission but the authorities refused it. So we were back where we began.

Some measure of resolution was then achieved.

" Now it has been agreed that all outside letting of the hall shall be discontinued, with the exception of the day classes of the LCC

Above: The church hall accounts for 1946. (St Luke's Church News)

January, 1962

throughout the year and the Post Office at Christmas. I am thankful to say that I have been able to obtain the LCC's agreement to a substantially increased rent.

However, in his letter in the parish magazine of January 1962, he describes the ongoing problems:

" The hall is still a liability. We are at the moment searching for the cause of the heavy rain leaks. The redecoration is urgent. Repairs will continue to arise. But at least we have got over what has been a continuing anxiety for a long time past. We have, we hope, settled the problem of St Luke's Hall.

The decision was made to redecorate the church and work began on 1 January 1962. However, it soon became clear that services could not continue to be held in the church, so a decision was made to hold services in the large church hall.

" Mr Preston with Mr Hopkins worked wonders and an altar was set on the stage, fully vested with cross and candles, seats for the clergy and servers, while the choir members sat facing each other at the foot of the stage. Flowers were everywhere to beautify it.

The vicar thought the closeness of the congregation

to the altar was a good thing and that it brought everyone closer together. When services returned to the church, the congregation was encouraged to avoid the back pews.

By October 1963 Rev Lambert was again at his wits' end as to what to do with the church hall.

" It ought never to have been bought. Last autumn the boiler repairs led to a loss of £94 on the year. Now we have a burst tank, frozen pipes and a repair bill of £100.

Again in March 1963 he posed the question: "Who would like to buy the church hall?" It was, he said, "proving a drain on resources, needs repairs, is less and less used and losing the church money every year". He went on to say how it would, with its five floors and many rooms, be ideal for offices. The price he stated "would be very reasonable".

The building was finally sold to Lambeth Council in 1965. After its sale the church continued to make some use of the hall, leasing it from Lambeth before moving into a new venue in October 1969.

Above: St Luke's Church News, January 1962. (LMA P85/LUK/143)

Opposite: The parish hall when SLTC took occupation, 1967. (SLT Archive)

CHAPTER FOUR

A theatre is born when SLTC is formed in 1967

Two local drama groups, the Lambeth Drama Club and the Proscenium Club, were both by chance looking for a new building for theatrical purposes and decided, in the mid-1960s, to combine their quest.

St Luke's Church Hall seemed a viable option, although it had lain disused for some time and was quite neglected. Despite this, it was thought worth investigating. Complex negotiations ensued, as well as discussions with Lambeth Borough Council and the Lambeth Arts and Recreation Association, which offered generous financial assistance with the rental of the building. Eventually, on 1 January 1967, members of the South London Theatre Project took possession of their new home, which was to be named the South London Theatre Centre.

THE CONVERSION BEGINS

With the help of a local architect, Owen Luder, plans were put together to convert the building into a theatre. Once his office had submitted these plans, thereafter his involvement seems to have been light, as the works were chiefly carried out by voluntary labour from within the SLTC's ranks.

To transform the plans into a solid theatrical structure, 50 or so members from the two founding clubs were faced with a vast amount of work, at an estimated cost of about £3,000. "Operation conversion" advanced along two broad fronts. Publicity and fundraising came first, followed by the transformation into an operational theatre.

One publicity stunt entailed unsuspecting local shoppers being accosted by a band of youthful looking pirates, while further along the street, a procession of haggard "prisoners" being whipped along the road by cheerful guards handing out publicity was surprisingly successful.

Opposite: Members of the SLTC take to the streets to drum up funds and support for the fledgling group, 1967. (SLT Archive)

First to be tackled on the building front was the bar area in the basement. Once constructed, it was a place where members could get together and nurse their blistered hands. It was finished just in time to hold the first annual general meeting in May 1967, at which point the membership stood at 140 people.

After the bar, work began on the theatre proper. The floor just above the main fire doors was removed and the joists used to form the basis of the new 12-inch-

Above: Original concept drawing for the first SLTC members' bar in pen and wash, 1967. (SLT Archive)

Left: The members' bar under construction. Features such as the stone-flagged floor from its previous use as a kitchen and wash-house were retained where possible, 1967. (SLT Archive)

Opposite: The finished members' bar was stylish, atmospheric and brimming with 1960s' chic. An appealing space which would become intrinsic to the club's identity, 1967. (SLT Archive)

high stage. Partition walls were erected to separate the theatre from the luncheon club room, and brick piers were built to support a raked auditorium, while the side of the building was modified to form the main entrance and foyer.

The entire building was rewired and work progressed to the upper storeys, where one room became a costume store, another a technicians' room and third a rehearsal room.

FOUNDING MEMBERS

COLIN STOKES

"I joined the Lambeth Drama Club in September 1966. I was always interested in theatre and the arts and thought this would be a good way to 'get involved'. From an electrical background, lighting issues were of particular interest. Soon after I joined, I learnt there was a project being put together between the Lambeth Drama Club and the Proscenium Club. The two companies formed the South London Theatre Centre, and we moved into the building remarkably quickly.

The building was not in the best of states and the basement was under about a foot of water. Work soon got under way to convert it into a functioning theatre, with the workforce consisting of existing

OWEN LUDER, CBE

Our "Honorary Architect", is now known throughout the world. He has been both president of the Royal Institute of British Architects and chairman of the Architects Registration Board, and is still active in a number of directorial roles, at the age of 89. The South London Theatre is proud to have welcomed him to a few gala performances at the theatre over the years.

members of the two clubs and many new members who were attracted to the project. The vast majority of the work was carried out by volunteers, although certain professional services had to be called upon. I was involved in many electrical areas, as well as general duties, including some bricklaying in the auditorium. It was very much 'all hands to the pump'. I spent many productive evenings there until we were ready to open with our first production of *The Alchemist* in October that year. Little has physically changed to the building since those early days, other than the creation of the Prompt Corner studio theatre.

I remained an active member of SLTC, lighting a considerable number of productions up until 1981 then rejoined about two years ago as an audience member when I retired."

Opposite: Work begins in earnest to create the fly loft, 1967. (Ted Neal)

CHARLIE CHEETHAM

Charlie first came through the big red doors as work was already under way and sees those early years from a different perspective.

"In March 1967 I was walking by the old fire station and the double doors were open, so I looked in. It was like a demolition site. In the darkness, a voice said: 'Can I help you?'

'Just being nosey. Came here as a kid for Sunday school,' I said, to where the voice came from. There was a guy sitting on a girder – the ceiling had gone.

'What are you doing?'

'Converting the building into a theatre.'

'On your own?'

'No, two drama groups have leased the building from Lambeth Council.'

"And that's how I met Ted Neal, one of the brains behind the project. My wife Ann and I joined the SLTC and soon involved ourselves with an enthusiastic membership. By this time the stage was taking shape, the rigging was up, and the lighting and sound were operated from the fly-loft. The auditorium was raked and the proscenium arch was built, while the seating came from the Astoria Cinema in Streatham.

"Sunday night was social night in the bar and was always packed. It was built on barrels and planks, and the seating was converted church pews.

"The area which is now Prompt Corner was turned into a luncheon club for the local pensioners, part of the terms of the lease agreed with Lambeth Council, which provided the meals and staff.

"For the next 20-odd years I was involved with acting, directing, working backstage and fundraising. We liked to spread the name of SLTC in those early years, entering both the Croydon and Lambeth drama festivals and winning them both. We took productions to Questors Theatre in Ealing, as well as to Falmouth and Bolton. I could write a book on the happenings and the wonderful people I got to know, who made such a valued contribution to SLTC in those early years."

As the building neared completion, rehearsals began for the first production and once the seating was installed in the auditorium, members realised they had built a theatre in just 10 months. A few coats of paint, a quick spring clean and the centre was ready to welcome its invited guests for the grand opening on 30 October 1967.

Opposite: SLTC's first production The Alchemist, 1967. (SLT Archive)

CHAPTER FIVE

Theatrical trials and titillations 1967-77

VIRGINIA WOOLF AND THE THREE-DAY WEEK

The miners' strike and the three-day week of the early 1970s left the consumption of electricity severely restricted. In December 1970, a production of *Who's Afraid of Virginia Woolf* by Edward Albee was staged, with Tina Kanarek and Vic Shaw in the lead roles. Half the performances were plunged into darkness, due to the lack of electricity, but the show still went on. It was already a powerful production, enhanced even further when the stage was lit by candlelight.

THE LONGEST PLAY ON RECORD

With power restrictions lifted, February 1972 brought the staging of the longest play in the theatre's history. *The Iceman Cometh* by Eugene O'Neill, the lead being played by Colm O'Neill, had a running time of about four hours including intervals, with the final curtain coming down at midnight – sadly too late for last orders at the bar.

STATUS UPDATE

After seven years of negotiations and the adoption of a changed constitution at the AGM in 1974-75, a fresh application was made to the Charity Commission, which agreed to register South London Theatre Centre Ltd as a charity.

The immediate advantage was that the theatre could apply for a reduction in rates and, in the long term, the new status would substantially help in the appeal for funds to build a new theatre or convert an existing building when the time came to move.

One of the conditions attached to the charitable status was that the SLTC Members' Club, which was responsible for the sales of intoxicating liquor, among other things, became a separate organisation. The bar remained in the basement, but now had a separate governing committee.

Opposite: The Iceman Cometh by Eugene O'Neill, 1972. (Bim Harding)

A year later it was reported that the theatre was now a limited company and since the registration as a charity, a 50 per cent reduction in the general rate had been achieved.

STUDIO THEATRE VS LUNCHEON CLUB

Towards the end of 1974, the theatre committee acknowledged a delay in setting up the new proposed studio theatre. The stumbling block appeared to be the luncheon club, which occupied the space during the day. At rehearsals the actors would try to guess what had been on the menu that day – stewed greens seemed to be a popular choice. Then, suddenly, the pensioners and the lingering luncheon smells were no more. It had been closed by Lambeth Council, although no explanation was given.

The theatre committee proposed starting work on the raised platforms for the seating, which would facilitate one-night shows starting in the new year. This second space became Prompt Corner and is described in more detail in Chapter Seven.

JOINING THE LITTLE THEATRE GUILD

In December 1975, Jimmy Morgan reported in the monthly newsletter that application had been made

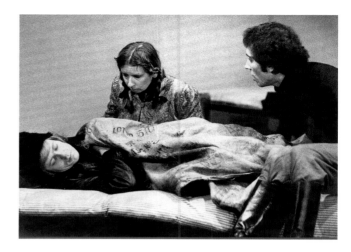

to join the Little Theatre Guild of Great Britain (LTG) and that the theatre had got through the preliminaries and was at the stage of having its quality assessed. One play, *The Promise*, had already been seen and admired, and *Mother Courage* would soon be seen as part of this process.

The application was successful and SLTC joined in 1976. The LTG is a collection of amateur theatres of a similar high standard spread all over the country, and regional conferences are held regularly.

Members of SLT have held important positions in the LTG, not least John Anderson, SLT's long-term chairman, who was national chairman of the LTG from 1995-97. Through John, the theatre was also represented at the International Theatre Exchange, the UK arm of the International Amateur Theatre Association. Ann Mattey was also national secretary of the LTG for more than 10 years.

Above: The Promise by Aleksei Arbuzov directed by Ann Parnell-McGarry, 1-7 November, 1975. (Bim Harding)

MODERN TAKE ON A GREEK CLASSIC

Male nudity hit the main stage in Laurence Staig's interpretation of the Greek tragedy *Agamemnon* in 1977. Bruce Murray, in the title role, was required to take a bath on stage (in which he was killed). Strobes illuminated the dimly lit stage, so the nudity was only glimpsed briefly, but it was still a first for SLTC. The murder was "brilliant and chilling", according to Donald Madgwick of the *Croydon Advertiser*. Not only was there a chorus of stick-wielding soldiers lining both sides of the auditorium, and human motorbikes on stage, but actors rowed to Troy on a ramp above the audience's heads – a memorable effect. Madgwick went on to say the production as a whole was "an all-out assault on the senses".

1977: TIN ANNIVERSARY

In 1977, a 10th-anniversary committee was set up to organise a whole year of special events, productions and fundraising, with the aim of raising £15,000.

Commencing on 31 December through to 8 January, including four matinées, the theatre delved for the first time into pantomime, with a production of *Aladdin*. This was followed on 16 January by a reception for local dignitaries, with a preview showing of *The Master of Two Servants*, which was then staged in Prompt Corner the following weekend.

Productions in 1977 included *The Prime of Miss Jean Brodie* and *You're a Good Man, Charlie Brown*. Jill Clarke directed a powerful production of *Macbeth*, with Colm O'Neill in the title role, as the anniversary show, exactly 10 years to the month after the theatre's first production.

The year was rounded off in December with a special production of *Sweeney Todd*, with Charlie Cheetham playing the demon barber of Fleet Street.

CHAPTER SIX

The Members' Club – the heart of SLT

As with many conversion projects, the basement was the first focus. This meant that the bar was installed first – not an easy task as it was under a foot of water at the time. Work soon got started, however, and the Members' Club officially opened in May 1967, using empty beer barrels and planks of wood for seating. Soon the acquisition of some local church pews and homemade tables added a more homey feel.

MORE THAN JUST A BAR

The Members' Club's primary function was always to give support to the theatre above. When, in 1974, the theatre attained charitable status, the bar had to be separated from the theatre, at least on paper, but the Members' Club continued to contribute to the theatre to the tune of about £10,000 a year. Providing drinks to theatre audiences before and after the show, as well as in the interval, the bar is also the social hub of the theatre, providing a space for rehearsals, auditions, meetings and social events.

The Members' Club is run by a committee of volunteers, ensuring the bar is fully stocked and planning and organising a whole host of social events throughout the year.

Throughout the 1970s and 1980s there were regular folk nights, showcasing home-grown talent, and quizzes were a popular feature, including the annual film quiz, that has continued to this day. Some of these events, such as Christmas and New Year parties, were so popular that tickets had to be issued.

One of the chairmen at this time was Bob Marshall, who acquired a full-size roulette table and introduced an annual casino night. For a small fee, members could purchase a wad of fake money and then play on the roulette table or at various other games such as poker, blackjack or craps. A prize was awarded to the person who managed to increase their fake money pile the most after a set period. With the games being

Opposite: Members enjoy the first SLTC bar, 1967 (SLT Archive)

run by members, and cocktails and glamorous attire being encouraged, this was always a popular event.

Peter Barker was the bar chairman at the time of the 25th anniversary in 1992. He wrote in the anniversary programme: "The social aspect of the bar covers anything from poetry readings, quiz nights and casinos nights, to variety shows … Our infamous party nights are always popular. Who could forget the Vicars and Tarts Ball, 'Back to School' and the sixties night, and the impromptu party night when the Czechoslovakian Touring Company, Chorea Bohemica, burst into song and danced in the bar, which must go down as one of our more memorable evenings."

A wide range of beers, wines, spirits and soft drinks is served in the bar which has been sponsored by both the Youngs and Fullers breweries.

Matthew Lyne, who has been involved with the running of the bar for many years, comments: "With an ever-increasing number of alternatives in up-and-coming West Norwood, the bar has had to be more responsive to the demands of the membership, while at the same time being able to cater for the varied tastes of our theatre audiences. On the social side, as well as the usual diet of quizzes and parties, new events such as evenings of stand-up comedy, under the banner of SLTee-Hee-Hee,

featuring some of the finest young comics around and MC'd by our own Simon Holland, have been staged in the bar itself. Film nights, karaoke evenings and even cake bake-offs have also been features of our social seasons."

The crowning glory of the bar room is its fabulous ceiling. Posters from productions have been pasted up over many years, and since 2007 every show is represented, right up to the final pre-restoration productions of *Edgar & Annabel* and *The Swan* in 2015. Every inch of it was photographed before it was dismantled with a view to replacing it in the refurbished building.

Many members of the theatre have also served on the committee of the Members' Club throughout its history, and its operation would not be possible without them.

Above: One of the many SLT Casino Nights, 1987. (Brian Fretwell)

Opposite: (clockwise) Winter folk night 1980, bar billiards in the green room 1985, SLT car rally away day 1991, Name That Play Party 1979. (Brian Fretwell)

CHAPTER SEVEN

Prompt Corner – the theatre gains a studio space 1975

Opening in February 1975, Prompt Corner became the South London Theatre's studio space, providing a second performance area that would be separate from, but complement, the main stage.

Charlie Cheetham, a founder member and part of the committee when Prompt Corner was being considered, recalls its inception.

"It was part of the agreement with Lambeth Council when we got the lease for the building that they would set up a luncheon club for 70 senior citizens. It ran for quite a while, until the council decided to close it towards the end of 1974. Theatre Committee lost no time in putting the space to good use, but it was Bert Lenny, our saviour, who was a member in his 70s and retired. During the day, single-handed, he cleared the rubbish that had accumulated, redecorated and, having carpentry skills, built raked seating to accommodate 40 or more people. For his efforts, the theatre made him an honorary member."

The first production mounted in the new space was *In Camera* by Jean-Paul Sartre, directed by Ann Parnell-McGarry. The production ran on 15 and 16 February of 1975 and tickets cost just 30p.

In the autumn of that year, Parnell-McGarry was appointed as the first administrator of Prompt Corner (PCA). She was the main instigator of the idea of starting a studio theatre and was heavily involved from the beginning in all the preparatory work, creating the structure and suggesting its name, so was the obvious candidate for the role. She took control of the project and transformed it into a workable, self-supporting theatre.

To drum up support and interest, she wrote in the newsletter: "This is an idea which has been in the minds of many of us for a long time. There have been attempts to get it off the ground but without great success. However, this time we are going to

Opposite: You're a Good Man, Charlie Brown, 1977. (SLT Archive)

This, our latest venture, was conceived as SHOP WINDOWS then grew into an idea of a LITTLE THEATRE, and now we proudly announce the birth of

THE PROMPT CORNER

We are bound to have teething troubles, unavoidable when working with nothing but the bare bones, operating on a shoestring. It is a platform for trying out new ideas, adapting well-tried old ones, and a proving ground for new talent. Actors and directors alike are able to express themselves by doing things that would not fit into the main theatre pattern, in a place where allied creative arts can be aired and mixed, where we can talk shop with local or outside experts on the practice and theory of the arts, or invite other theatres to show us what they are doing and thinking about. Most important of all - you can join in.

Dear audience - we need your patience, support, opinions and ideas (only signed abuse will be accepted). The standard will vary, but we hope to be always interesting and sometimes exciting. Your comments will be welcome - don't be shy - not just extreme comments, tell us about the little things you dislike or were intrigued about, and all those you liked as well.

It is a black box theatre and as such has no fixed seating, so its configuration is only limited by the director's imagination. That said, as a studio theatre every aspect of the show is meant to be kept as simple as possible and that is reflected by the smaller amount of time a show is given to set up the theatre.

The first Prompt Corner programme, 1975. (SLT Archive)

make a success of it and create much more activity in the club. ... It will be an adaptable theatre so that there can be the conventional proscenium performances and performance in the round. For the proscenium productions there will be raked seating with a capacity of 44. For in-the-round performances seating will be at floor level and have a capacity of almost 60. There will be some productions that will run for two nights on Saturday and Sunday and some for one night only on a Sunday. We envisage that the two-nighters will be used for new directors, new plays, full-length plays and one-act plays (to form a double bill); and the one-night stands for experimental theatre, mime, improvisation, dance, audience participation, excerpts from plays and dramatisation of literature and poetry. ... The scheme is open to everyone who would like to direct. Our most experienced directors might like to tackle some unfamiliar or experimental play. On the acting front, perhaps you have not yet managed a part on the main stage, but have experience elsewhere, well, now is your chance. ... This theatre is being encouraged in order to supplement the main theatre and not to detract from it. As always the main theatre comes first – but if you are not currently involved and want to be, then we want to know."

Prompt Corner was officially opened in September 1975 with a production of *The Clerk's Account* written by member John Yorath, featuring John Harris in a riveting solo performance.

The new space ran its affairs on a modest budget, putting on productions to supplement the main stage season, succeeding in attracting professional performers and playing host to visiting speakers. Other activities included the writers' circle, youth drama workshops on a Saturday morning and classes about theatrecraft held by professional tutors.

Ann had the support of Bob Skinner, Tony Westhead and Jimmy Morgan (among others) in planning the venture, with Bert Lenny and Bernie Bullbrook helping with the building and rigging, and many other volunteers. However, a few members expressed concern that it would drain acting talent from the main theatre, and was maybe too ambitious.

The PCA had a large, complicated brief to fulfil, and Ann had already worked for months on every aspect of the preparation necessary. She created a huge amount of publicity for the new venture long before it opened, with the help of Malcolm Johnson, a professional photographer. Ann was keen to run it like a professional fringe theatre – events were planned for every available weekend, with the venue attracting a diverse range of acts and audiences. It was an exciting, innovative, but time-consuming and exhausting project.

Above: Female Transport by Steve Gooch, Prompt Corner, 1982.
    (SLT Archive)

A MORE FORMAL FOOTING

Parnell-McGarry accomplished a great deal in her tenure, and Prompt Corner showcased 30 productions in that first year alone, after which Mark Powell took over. By the beginning of 1976, a set of rules and regulations for the new theatre had been prepared. The following six aims were laid down.

Prompt Corner exists to:

1. Present all forms of entertainment suitable to its place with special emphasis on the sort of attraction not usually put on in the main theatre, eg music, poetry, dance, lectures, experimental and short plays, films, etc
2. Expand facilities available to members
3. Find and expose new producers, actors and technical staff
4. Give opportunities to experienced producers, actors and technical staff to do something different from their usual work
5. Present new plays of quality
6. Fill "open" weekends with shows.

This continued to put a lot of pressure on the PCA and the quality of work produced was not always consistent, but there were some striking successes. The *Fantasticks*, an intimate opera by Harvey Schmidt and Tom Jones, was so well received that it had to be

repeated; *Oddi Orri*, a brand-new rock musical by Roger Haines, Gerald Campbell and James Dillon, attracted capacity audiences during a heatwave, despite an auditorium temperature of 104F; while a "coarse acting" version of Wilde's *The Importance of Being Earnest* left people holding their sides.

In the summer of 1976, a "pay what you like" system called Almost Free was introduced to Prompt Corner, and takings went up. Although the new payment system did not last, it was a sign of the innovative way that the studio was ready to operate. Despite some teething troubles, Prompt Corner went from strength to strength and became an important fixture in the life of the theatre.

FAMOUS FACES

A series of famous speakers was booked to entertain audiences on Sunday evenings, although not all of these appeared in the studio. One was the actress

Above: Beryl Reid with her cat, 1973. (Photograph © Alan Warren)

Beryl Reid who, after some recordings of her work were played, was interviewed about her career, performed some of her famous pieces and took part in a question-and-answer session.

Other visitors, booked via Prompt Corner, appeared on the main stage, including Quentin Crisp in 1977, who proved to be an entertaining, thought-provoking and memorable guest, offering a variety of anecdotes, the subject of his talk being "style", and entitled *A Straight Talk from a Bent Speaker*. The film *The Naked Civil Servant*, starring John Hurt, had just come out, and it was the eve of the publication of the paperback of his autobiography, so an informal book signing took place afterwards in the bar.

Above: Quentin Crisp in New York City, 1992. (Ross Bennett Lewis)

Sam Wanamaker, Sheridan Morley, Michael Green and Nicholas de Jongh have also spoken, creating lively and stimulating evenings in very good company.

A WINNING FORMULA

Initially, directors were only allowed to direct a play on the main stage if they had put one on in Prompt Corner first, which gave the committee the chance to monitor the output and keep standards high.

Gradually the number of performances increased and the Saturday/Sunday night productions became three-nighters, finishing on the Saturday night. Over time, three nights became four and eventually Prompt Corner productions had equal status to those on the main stage, usually performing for five nights on the third week of the month.

You're a Good Man, Charlie Brown (1977), the musical, was initially put on in Prompt Corner for two nights in the April and when a main stage production fell through, the director Bruce Murray was asked to restage it to fill the five-night main-stage slot in October. It also represented the theatre at an "in the round" festival, and again at the Ashcroft Theatre in Croydon for another festival. Two actors from the original cast made it to all four venues.

DIFFERENT DESIGNS

The original idea of Prompt Corner was to keep things as simple as possible with open staging and no set. While many productions have been done successfully this way, the space has proved its flexibility, with numerous types of sets being constructed, and the seating adapted for different configurations.

From early on several modern classics were staged in Prompt Corner, such as the 1976 production of Samuel Beckett's *Endgame*, with moving performances from John Lyne as Hamm and Terry Floyd as Clov.

In *Palach*, by Alan Burns and Charles Marowitz, in 1978, the actors performed in the round on three stages simultaneously, with the audience immersed in the action.

Prompt Corner gave the first amateur production of (SLT member) Bill Moody's play *Sunburnt Ears* in 1987, which was first performed at The Cottlesloe, National Theatre, in 1986. Two further versions of this poignant and moving play were also shown at SLT in 1994 and 1995.

Under Milk Wood by Dylan Thomas has had three productions, two of them in Prompt Corner. The 1991 version was the first time the set extended the length of the space, with Captain Cat's "eyrie" high

above the audience and the shore for the fishing boats at the opposite end. The last production, in 2004, pared everything back to the original concept of a "play for voices" using six actors on separate rostra, with spotlights linking them.

Never forgetting that pure entertainment and fun are an important part of the mix, a 6ft actor played a five-year-old in the *The Golden Pathway Annual* (1983), while *Nunsense* (1993) starred five singing nuns.

Above: Endgame, 1976. (Hand-painted poster by Jeanette Hoile)

*Above: Prompt Corner is transformed from a cottage to a graveyard in
Martin McDonagh's A Skull in Connemara, 2012. (Phil Gammon)*

Complicated sets don't appear as often in the studio as on the main stage, but one director who pulled off an intricately designed staging was Naomi Liddle, for her 2012 production of Martin McDonagh's *A Skull in Connemara*.

"The ingenuity of SLT set designers knows no bounds," she explains. "The play requires the action to move seamlessly from a ramshackle Irish country living room to a graveyard at night, complete with diggable graves. To achieve this, Chaz Doyle built a raised stage, cunningly hiding two graves containing a full tonne of earth beneath the 'floorboards' of the living room. A quick lift of the 'lids' and our central character was revealed, apparently up to his waist in a grave, mid-dig. The smell of earth wafted over the audience as our long-suffering actor knelt in the hole and shifted shovelful after shovelful of mud.

"The same show also necessitated the moulding of more than 50 plaster-of-Paris bones and skulls, which were smashed to smithereens each night. My kitchen was transformed into an ossuary for weeks in advance as we painstakingly crafted our doomed skeletons. *A Skull in Connemara* remains for me a perfect example of the amazingly high production levels that South London Theatre can achieve on a shoestring, fuelled by enthusiasm, ingenuity and raw talent. And it was a hell of a good craic!"

One of the funniest and raunchiest shows that Prompt Corner has produced – *Saucy Jack and the Space Vixens* by Charlotte Mann (2010) – set the audience inside a seedy nightclub in a future universe and planet. Involving fabulous costumes and a catchy disco track, the show was enhanced by a sign language interpreter, Paul Michaels, who managed to make it even funnier than it already was. Sign language interpretation has featured in several SLT shows.

For *Trainspotting*, in 2010, the actors climbed on scaffolding, close to the ceiling, and mingled with the audience at ground level during a promenade production. In *There is a War* in 2014, a cast of 14 used scaffolding again, plus a variety of scenery and levels to keep the promenade audience on its feet, trying to predict where the cast would appear from next.

Neither have difficult subjects been avoided, such as the oppressive political regime of *Death and the Maiden*

(2003) and the effects of paedophilia in *Blackbird* (2010), while offering a taste of the unusual in plays such as Sam Shepard's *Tooth of Crime* (2014).

Originally, the intention was to use the space for a range of plays that was more experimental, less well-known, or newer but challenging, and Prompt Corner has always offered an eclectic and sometimes provocative mix.

The studio space has more than earned its keep since its inception and has become an integral and important part of the theatre's output.

Above left: Saucy Jack and the Space Vixens, 2010. (Phil Gammon)

Above right: The bleak, disused office from Blackbird, 2010. (Phil Gammon)

Opposite: Trainspotting, 2010. The studio became a dark and dank bedsit made from stark scaffold poles with television screens punching through the oppressive gloom. (Becan Rickard-Elliot)

CHAPTER EIGHT

A long and tireless history of fundraising

CHARITY EVENTS

As a charity, South London Theatre has spent a lot of time during its history fundraising in a variety of ways.

THE MAIN STAGE GETS A NAME

On 29 May 1981, the main stage was officially named the Bell Theatre. The same day the 48-hour Shakespeare Marathon began (see right), and was the first production under the new name. West Norwood Fire Brigade joined in the naming ceremony, together with the Red Cross and Lambeth's deputy mayor. The Fire Brigade donated a genuine fire bell to the theatre, which was installed in the bar and used to make announcements or call time from then on. The renaming ceremony was heralded by coverage on Radio London, Capital Radio and LBC, with TV coverage on BBC's *Nationwide* and *Thames News*.

48-HOUR SHAKESPEARE MARATHON – 1981

Organised by Ann Mattey, this involved teams of actors and Shakespeare enthusiasts, working through as many Shakespeare plays as they could, either reading or improvising a performance. Each team was on stage for four hours and off for about six, which often meant that participants slept on the floor of the rehearsal room. Other teams and members were supportive and went to watch when *Titus Andronicus* was performed at 4am and the women of one team rebelled at the paucity of roles available so *Romeo and Juliet* was performed with the genders reversed. The aim, however, to read all the plays in 48 hours, proved impossible – Shakespeare was just too prolific. However, 23 plays were completed – a respectable number – and £1,900 was raised.

Several current and future professional actors such

Opposite: Members of the West Norwood Fire Brigade turn out for the renaming ceremony of Bell Theatre, 1981. (SLT Archive)

as Fred Ridgeway, Angie Shrubsole, Adrian McLoughlin and Alan McMahon were involved, with the *Croydon Advertiser* critic Donald Madgwick popping in to enjoy the atmosphere.

A BUMPER RAFFLE – 1980s

Members donated a variety of prizes, of which the top one was a car or its monetary equivalent. Raffle books were posted to all members with their newsletters and sold well. On the day of the grand draw, the top prize winner John Cooke – a loyal and supportive member of the club – generously donated the money back to the theatre.

BRICKS FOR SALE – 1980s

SLT bricks were sold, although there was no way to identify which had been bought – just a warm glow from knowing that the theatre had benefited.

PERSONALISED THEATRE SEATS – 1992

Every seat in the Bell Theatre was made available for sale. Once bought, a small plaque with the buyer's name on it was attached to that seat. Some of these could still be found on the seats in 2015, before they were sold prior to the refurbishment. Others didn't last quite so long. Several famous benefactors bought a seat, including Frankie Howerd, who lived locally and had visited the theatre a few times; Alan Ayckbourn, who always supported amateur theatres with fundraising efforts; and Jane Merrow, best known for her role in 1968's *The Lion in Winter*, and daughter of Bill Merrow, himself a respected director, actor and active SLT member.

MARATHON EFFORTS

Several energetic members have taken part in marathons, half marathons and other sporting events in aid of theatre funds. Among these are Neil Husband, Fleur Hogarth, Anton Krause, Andrew Chadney and Jess Osorio.

OTHER EVENTS

Quizzes, cake sales, cabarets, casino nights, folk nights, comedy shows, auctions and many raffles have all contributed to the theatre's coffers.

Opposite: (clockwise) 48-hour Shakespeare marathon readings take place on Bell Stage 1981; taking a break from the 48-hour Shakespeare marathon 1981; juggling while running the Wimbledon 10k 2003; the seat bought by the 1979 Writers Circle in 1992. (Brian Fretwell, Bryon Fear)

CHAPTER NINE

Home-grown talent – new writing at the theatre

THE WRITERS' CIRCLE

For many years, the theatre had a "writers' circle" formed in May 1976, to encourage members to write original plays, a few of which were published after their South London Theatre premieres. Valerie Elliott and Ken Lucas were involved with the group for some years and gave many budding playwrights the chance to hear and see their work in action. At first, a few of the Writers' Circle plays were performed together in rehearsed readings by fellow members, often in the bar or in Prompt Corner. Later, some longer plays were given full performances in Prompt Corner. Some early writers were Val Elliott, John Yorath, Chris O'Shaughnessy, Ken Lucas and Mike Schirn.

THE CRYSTAL PALACE FIRE

A notable production from the Writers' Circle was *The Last Day of November* by John Yorath. As deputy head of a local school, John often wrote plays for his pupils and he adapted this one for the South London Theatre. It traced the history of the Crystal Palace, from the Great Exhibition in Hyde Park to its relocation in Sydenham, culminating in the night of the famous fire. The irony of performing a play about a famous fire inside a fire station was not lost on many of those involved.

As dress rehearsal week approached, John had to be frisked for pencils at each rehearsal, while constantly honing his script. All the scenes portrayed real characters and events, while illuminating contributions from people of all walks of life.

His script was matched by the vision of the director, Bruce Murray, whose design of an all-white Victorian set featured black shading, often using cross-hatching, as seen in drawings of the time. Buildings and fountains were depicted, as well as the famous naked statues, which had shocked some

Opposite: The Last Day of November, 1983. (SLT Archive)

of the Victorian visitors. Only rear views of the nudes were seen, but were drawn from life.

Against this monochrome background, Bruce had the Victorian-style costumes made in jewel-bright primary colours, creating a striking impact. In the final scene of the 30 November 1936 fire, the actors wore original tunics and helmets from the period, with flames flickering in the darkness and a screen showing 1936 *Pathé News* film footage of the fire.

The Crystal Palace Foundation (CPF) allowed John free access to its archives and enabled SLT to produce one of its most memorable programmes, with a booklet containing photographs of the history of the Crystal Palace, inside a cover featuring a historic drawing of the palace in all its glory.

There were two main productions of the play. The first, as above, in February 1983, was also taken to Questors Theatre, and in December 1984 it was restaged with a slightly different cast and set. The script is still available in the CPF shop on Anerley Hill.

CONTINUED SUPPORT FOR NEW WRITERS

After this, playwrights operated independently, or their plays were performed under the title of "new writers' showcases". Recently, new writing has been produced in both Bell Theatre and Prompt Corner, and has been a regular part of most years' seasons.

In latter years plays by Stuart Draper, Mark Bullock, Matthew Davies, Jenny Gammon, Rodney Quinn and Eddie Coleman have all been showcased, as well as many short pieces by Alan Buckman. Member Bill Moody was a professional actor and is the only SLT playwright to have had one of his plays, *Sunburnt Ears*, performed professionally at the Cottesloe, National Theatre, in 1986, before SLT gave the first amateur performances in 1987. The play also went on to have successful runs at the King's Head, Islington, and the Edinburgh Festival in 1992.

Above: Stiff by Matthew Davies, 2009. (Phil Gammon)

Opposite: 4Play by Eddie Coleman, 2011. (Phil Gammon)

CHAPTER TEN

South London Theatre and the bard – the play's the thing

The works of William Shakespeare have played a huge role in the theatre's 50-year history. Some of his plays have been produced three or four times, while others such as the theatre's Shakespearean debut *Pericles*, have only made solo appearances.

TWELFTH NIGHT

The first outing for this play was in 1969, and was a traditional production, with lots of ruffs, doublets and hose. Its next appearance wasn't until December 2001 when, in keeping with the title, it was set at Christmas and produced with lots of Rennie Mackintosh flair.

MUCH ADO ABOUT NOTHING

Proving its timeless popularity, *Much Ado* has been seen on the South London Theatre stage three times. The first of these was in May 1971, with Ruth Lidyard and John Anderson in the main roles of Beatrice and Benedick. It was not revived until February 2000, with a modern-dress production directed by Matthew Bartlett, with Helen Chadney and James Newall in the roles of the bickering lovers. In its latest incarnation, in July 2014, a cunningly designed set enabled Alistair Mackay, as Benedick, to secrete himself in the branches of a scaffolding "tree", and the setting of soldiers returning from the conflict in Korea in 1949 gave plenty of opportunities for the use of swing and jive music.

MACBETH

Jill Clark took the reins for the first production of *Macbeth* in November 1977, which was also the theatre's 10th-anniversary show. Colm O'Neill and Midge Adams played the titular couple and period costumes were made by final-year students at Goldsmiths College. In the centre of the stage was a large sloping

Opposite: Pericles, 1968. (SLT Archive)

dais, around which a technically quite difficult final Macbeth-Macduff fight scene took place.

In 1980 the Scottish play made its second appearance, this time in Prompt Corner, directed by Ian Vallender. A pentangle was painted on the floor and every superstition was challenged.

Macbeth's next appearance in Prompt Corner in December 2004 was given a very different approach. Anton Krause, the director, explains: "*Macbeth* is about one man's ambition driving him into a downward spiral of violence until it consumes all those around him." The play was set in the present and contained no supernatural elements at all. The witches were voices in Macbeth's head and represented the darker half of his psyche. Krause's vision was that of a modern organised-crime family with Duncan at the head and Macbeth, Banquo, et al, as his captains. Krause continues: "This setting allowed us to replicate the hierarchical structure and the context of family and succession essential to the plot. It also explains why people kill each other..."

In May 2015 the Thane of Cawdor was back again, in what would be the final Shakespeare play before the refurbishment. Director Bryon Fear created this atmospheric piece with illustrative projections and a few stage blocks on an open stage. He also used an interesting twist having the witches played by children. Macbeth and his wife were played by Alistair Mackay and Audrey Lindsay, and the cast included some of the theatre's most experienced members such as Matthew Lyne (Duncan), Chaz Doyle (Macduff), Jeanette Hoile (Hecate), Malcolm Woodman (Doctor), Anita Sollis (Gentlewoman) and Alan Jarvis (Siward).

Above left: Macbeth, 1977 (Malcolm Johnson)

Above right: Macbeth, 2015 (Phil Gammon)

A MIDSUMMER NIGHT'S DREAM

A latecomer to the South London Theatre stages, an imaginative and magical modern-dress production of *A Midsummer Night's Dream* was directed by Jill Clark in July 1980, but was not then seen again until July 1997, in a production directed by John Mead. A more mature band of fairies, led by Ruth Lidyard as Titania and John Lyne as Oberon, gave the production a twist. A third production in October 2007, directed by Chaz Doyle, transformed the forests of Athens into a large warehouse in New York, and the fairies had metamorphosed into vampires, while the Youth Theatre gave it a colourful new spin in 2010.

THE MERCHANT OF VENICE

Another play that has seen three radically different productions, *The Merchant of Venice* was first aired in April 1982, in a traditional period piece, with Adrian McLoughlin trying to get his pound of flesh as Shylock. Seventeen years later, in 1999, Jack King chose the Venice of Mussolini's heyday as the backdrop for his production, while in 2011 Stuart Draper set his piece in 1943, during the Nazi occupation of Italy, which provided some chilling moments.

THE MERRY WIVES OF WINDSOR

The Merry Wives of Windsor has only appeared once, but it was the 25th-anniversary production, directed by Jill Clark, and an A4 glossy brochure was produced which included the show's programme in its centrefold. Alongside adverts from

Above left: A Midsummer Night's Dream, 1980. (SLT Archive)

Above right: The Merchant of Venice, 2011. (Phil Gammon)

businesses, there were articles about the bar, the youth and training departments, as well as how an SLT production is put together. A foreword from the chairman, John Anderson, explained: "It is the most exciting moment I know – the unknown journey of a play, or a new production of a much-loved play, is about to start. The stage is set where SLTC can, and will, for many years to come, entertain the eager and expectant playgoer."

THE COMEDY OF ERRORS

Two productions, first in 1996 and then in 2010, both had modern settings, the main difference being that the 1996 production had only two actors playing both sets of twins from Syracuse and Ephesus. They had to be very fit to manage the speedy costume changes and multiple entrances and exits. In 2010, however, there were two sets of actors playing the dual Antipholus and Dromio characters, though the pace was equally speedy, and confusion abounded.

MEASURE FOR MEASURE

A brace of productions of *Measure for Measure*, in 1997 and 2009, were both presented on the Bell stage, and were equally dark in content, highlighting themes of

morality and hypocrisy, although lightened by the comedy scenes of Mistress Overdone.

AND THE REST...

The following plays have graced the boards only once at the South London Theatre to date:

1968 – *Pericles*
1973 – *Hamlet*
1986 – *Coriolanus*
1994 – *The Taming of the Shrew*
2002 – *Two Gentlemen of Verona, Othello*
2003 – *The Tempest*
2004 – *Romeo and Juliet*
2006 – *Richard III*
2007 – *Julius Caesar*
2008 – *The Winter's Tale, King Lear*
2012 – *As You Like It*
2013 – *Timon of Athens*
2014 – *Henry V*
2017 – *Love's Labour's Lost*

Above: The Comedy of Errors, 1996. (Phil Gammon)

Opposite: Richard III, 2006. (Phil Gammon)

CHAPTER ELEVEN

Adding strings to bows – musical theatre at SLT

EARLY OVERTURES

The South London Theatre's productions have always reflected the strengths of the membership, and this is especially noticeable where musicals are concerned. In the early years, music-hall evenings would appear occasionally, and shows would be put on to celebrate Christmas, often with poetry and song. The first full-scale musical to be performed was *Oliver!* in 1975, directed by Ann Mattey. *The Fantasticks* and *Aladdin* followed, both directed by Lawrie Kenton.

THE WIZARD OF NZ

However, it wasn't until New Zealander Bruce Murray joined that the theatre's musical heyday arrived. Bruce offered two styles of musical theatre – the crowd-pleasing and entertaining large-cast shows such as *The Wizard of Oz* (1979), *Pippin* (1980), *Finian's Rainbow* (1984) and *Godspell* (1984),

and the intimate revue-style of *Rogers – A Man on the Great White Way* (1978), *Sing Brel* (1979), *Berlin to Broadway with Kurt Weill* (1982), and *Starting Here, Starting Now* (1983), all showcasing SLT's strong singers. He also directed 1977's *You're a Good Man, Charlie Brown*. The show proved that it had stood the test of time when Lisa Thomas' 2011 production was also a big hit with audiences.

Other notable shows were *Sweeney Todd the Barber* (1978), *Oh! What a Lovely War* (1979 and 2012), *Fing's Ain't Wot They Used T'Be* (1985), *Dames at Sea* (1985), *Gypsy* (1986), *Sweet Charity* (1987), *The Boy Friend* (1993 and 2013), *Nunsense* (1993 and 2015), *Cabaret* (1996), *A Slice of Saturday Night* (1998 and 2008), *Tomfoolery* (2006), *Elegies for Angels, Punks and Raging Queens* (2008), *Saucy Jack and the Space Vixens* (2010) and *The Kiss of the Spider Woman* (2012), along with pantomimes and other Christmas productions.

Opposite: Oh! What a Lovely War, 1979 and 2012.
(Above, Malcolm Johnson – below, Phil Gammon)

Little Shop of Horrors, in 2013, displayed the skills of the props team, who created an amazing set of "Audrey II" bloody-thirsty plants. *Oliver!* was the first Christmas show based at Stanley Halls and then, in August 2016, a stunning production of *Jesus Christ Superstar* was directed by Bryon Fear.

Often the early productions would use simply a pianist to accompany the singers. While some shows are still done this way, more musicians have often been added, usually gleaned from the membership, and in recent years, several shows have had a full band, together with actors using head microphones.

This culminated in the full rock-opera experience for *Jesus Christ Superstar*, courtesy of a talented band who were onstage throughout, under the musical direction of Gerard Johnson, accompanying a huge cast of singers, as they delivered a memorable show in a remarkable setting. The cavernous Stanley Halls was divided with a catwalk thrust stage, overlooked by Pilate's palace on the balcony above.

Above left: Elegies for Angels, Punks and Raging Queens, 2008. (Phil Gammon)

Above right: Little Shop of Horrors, 2013. (Siobhán Campbell)

Opposite: Jesus Christ Superstar, 2016. (Gaz de Vere)

CHAPTER TWELVE

Training & Youth Theatre – looking to the future

Teaching people about drama, and particularly teaching children, creates actors for the future and helps to keep the life blood of the theatre flowing. Drama can help the shyest individuals to come out of their shells, improve their social skills and give them a broader sense of self – and this is what drama training at SLT has always aimed to do.

TRAINING AND WORKSHOPS

SLT provided training classes for adults almost from its inception in 1967. Originally organised under the auspices of the South Lambeth Adult Education Institute, the classes included drama, stage design, stage lighting and costume, although the actor training was the most successful. AGM minutes from 1968 report that drama classes were well-established, with an average attendance of 18, while at least six lighting technicians had been trained. Eileen Pasco, who, along with Tina Kanarek, taught drama from the late 1960s onwards, reported that while some

people chose to attend classes regularly, others looked in occasionally meaning that continuity was often hard to achieve. Despite this, student productions were a regular part of the SLT programme, appearing at least once a year into the 1980s and allowing new actors the chance to display their learning.

THE YOUTH THEATRE

Drama classes for children date from somewhat later, in the early 1980s, but have proved far longer-lasting. Starting with one small class a week, they swiftly grew to several classes a week, organised by age group and taught during term time on Saturdays. Classes are not restricted to the children of members and those attending are not strictly local to the area – many come from

Opposite: Macbeth, 2015; children are not allowed to perform on consecutive nights, so this production had two sets of witches. (Káit Feeney)

considerably further afield. The aim was to help children to develop ways to express themselves and aid their communication skills – and also to have fun.

Nowadays the classes are taught by tutors with a range of skills and knowledge of different age groups. They are paid expenses but give their time willingly to provide a valuable experience for the children. The fees that come from youth classes have long been a valuable addition to the theatre's funds.

Children come to drama classes for all kinds of reasons. Many are genuinely starstruck and enjoy pretending to be someone else. Others love the social aspect – of learning something new alongside making new friends. One of the great benefits of learning to act at SLT is the opportunity to work in a real theatre alongside adult actors. For

many years, a full-length youth show has been programmed as part of the season, allowing older children to perform not just in front of their peers and parents but in front of an audience of "unknown" adults as well.

At other times, child actors are needed in adult plays and those with the desire to do so can audition for these roles, often gaining huge self-confidence from the experience and putting their adult counterparts to shame by their facility with line-learning and commitment. Recent adult shows requiring child actors have included quite challenging plays such as *Burnt by the Sun* (a whole

Above left: A Midsummer Night's Dream, 2010. (Phil Gammon)

Above right: Festen, 2015. (Phil Gammon)

troop of Young Pioneers, plus a lead role), *Cat on a Hot Tin Roof*, *The Accrington Pals* and *Festen*. In the opening scene of *Macbeth* (2015) three tall silhouetted witches turned to reveal that they were in fact children on stage blocks hidden by their long cloaks, in a striking coup de théâtre. And there is always the possibility of taking part in a musical such as *Oliver!* or a pantomime like *The Piper, Snow White and the Seven Dwarfs* and most recently *Jack* – the next chapter in the story of Jack and the Beanstalk.

Some children have had the opportunity to work outside the SLT theatre spaces – most memorably in *Stay With Me* (2006), a dark and harrowing double bill set during the Second World War, written by Stuart Draper. With the first half set in a concentration camp, and the second in a bombed-out school cellar, the plays dealt with important and complex issues. As well as being performed at the Old Fire Station, the plays transferred to the Greenwich Playhouse where they were performed to acclaim, giving their talented casts a chance to reach a far wider audience. More recently, the group took a truly scary production of Marlowe's *Doctor Faustus* into the cavernous space of St Luke's Church, West Norwood.

Not just for learning, not just for fun, youth drama gives children valuable skills, experience of acting and interacting with adults and a chance to find a new way to express and be themselves.

Above left: The Accrington Pals, 2015. (Phil Gammon)

Above right: Doctor Faustus, 2016. (Bryon Fear)

CHAPTER THIRTEEN

Through the wardrobe and beyond ...

Anyone who has ever visited the SLT wardrobe at the Old Fire Station with its packed rails, ranging across the centuries from ancient times to the present day, will have experienced its own special magic. The theatre costumes almost all the 15–24 shows it presents every year primarily from its own wardrobe and is able to offer them to other companies as well to create authentic looks for their own productions.

GRAND ORIGINS

The collection dates from the earliest days of the theatre and some of the costumes themselves from well before that. Iris Lenny started the wardrobe almost from the theatre's inception in 1967, with Ann Mattey taking over in the early 1970s. The two founding companies had some of their own items which they brought with them and over the years the collection was added to, with other items bought from clothing stock sales from professional companies such as the Royal Opera House and the National Theatre. Frequently SLT's wardrobe manager was invited to peruse the wardrobes of ladies who had been stylish dressers in the 1920s, 1930s and 1940s and was able to take away exquisite couture-quality dresses.

Today the collection spans the centuries, from tunics suitable for ancient Romans or Greeks, to medieval tabards and armour. There are Elizabethan doublets, Georgian menswear, Victorian crinolines and bustle cages and a huge range of menswear including uniforms that span the 19th and 20th centuries. The 20th-century treasure trove of womenswear includes lace and embroidered dresses and tailored suits from the 1930s to the 1960s – many of which would have been the height of fashion at the time they were made. There is also hand-stitched lingerie from the 1920s and 1930s.

Opposite: Top hats as worn by many an Artful Dodger. (Phil Gammon)

As well as these acquisitions, the theatre has frequently made costumes for its own shows. Alan Buckman, who trained as a theatrical costumier and worked at Glyndebourne opera house for a period, made a succession of superb period dresses. Cutting always on a dress form rather than using a pattern – and using fabrics from local markets, he created superb facsimiles of frocks from a range of different periods – the most recent was an exquisite Queen Anne dress for the play *Brandy* in 2010. Frequently cast as the dame in panto, Alan would also make at least five or six outfits for himself for every show, including fluorescent fur-trimmed medieval gowns – the results can still be seen on the pantomime rail.

For some shows, the costumes were created as a set and remain together. Past productions for which all the costumes were created specifically include *The Bacchae*, *A Midsummer Night's Dream*, *An Italian Straw*

Hat, *The Last Day of November*, *The Elephant Man*, *The Man Who Came to Dinner*, *The Merry Wives of Windsor*, *Lear's Daughters*, *Mort* and *Les Liaisons Dangereuses*. More recently the theatre produced a complete set of 18th-century naval and military coats for *Our Country's Good*, and a set of military-style jackets for *Macbeth*, while other productions have required the making of a "crocodile coat" and a full Victorian

Above left: Henry V, 2014. (Phil Gammon)

Above right: Lear's Daughters, 1993. (Brian Fretwell)

bustle outfit. And of course there are the pantos, which have needed (among other things) a whole set of medieval tunics, seven dwarfs, a pied piper and Dick Whittington's cat, reimagined as a smart-mouthed puppet.

Ann ran the wardrobe so successfully that, when she left London in 1985, a group of four helpers was needed to replace her, which it did for a year or so. After a while, Frances Walker was the only one remaining, and continued finding and hiring out costumes for numerous productions for many years.

Val Williams joined Frances in the SLT wardrobe in 1988 when her son was cast in *The Lion, the Witch and the Wardrobe*. Val is very knowledgeable about period costume, and her invaluable advice has been sought by many outside companies, as well as in-house. She is also able to improvise costumes and add the detail that gives a period flavour to more modern clothing. After Frances moved away, Val took over the management of the wardrobe and organised it very successfully, providing the theatre with a significant source of income, while at the same time making the SLT name known far and wide. Jess Osorio and Jenny Bennett have since continued the excellent work.

However, Val's most treasured moments have involved the making of a range of inspired props. These have

Above left: Ring Around the Moon, 1976. (SLT Archive)
Above right: Tom Jones, 2006. (Phil Gammon)

included a unicorn, a camel made for the pantomime *Aladdin*, a Jersey cow, wings for the angel in *Skellig*, a Harry Potter sorting hat, remote-controlled rats, a giant – and, perhaps best of all, an animatronic moose head. Most of these items are created in the first instance from papier-maché and many have eyes that move and realistic eyelashes. For the moose, Val recalls sketching real moose heads at the Horniman Museum depository and then crafting the antlers from coat hangers. The whole thing was operated like a puppet – the antlers could go up and down and revolve, the ears could flop and the eyelids could be opened and closed.

WELL WORN AND WELL TRAVELLED

The hiring of costumes to other groups has been a rich seam of income for the theatre and SLT costumes go out to many other amateur, fringe and professional companies, both theatrical and operatic, as well as to schools and are also hired by individual performers.

SLT's costumes have been seen in many BBC and ITV television drama documentaries and in touring productions of *A Midsummer Night's Dream* and *Romeo and Juliet*. They have also been seen on stage at Shakespeare's Globe and at the Edinburgh Festival

as well as in European tours of *Robinson Crusoe* and *Pinocchio* and in several films and videos.

As part of the Heritage Lottery Fund projects associated with the restoration of the Old Fire Station, members from the University of the Third Age spent months photographing and cataloguing SLT's wardrobe stock, organising it into eras and taking detailed measurements.

The restoration of the building and the relocation of the wardrobe will enable all the costumes to be organised in a more structured way and allow visiting actors, directors and designers to be shown the huge range of items on offer.

Above: The animatronic moose from the 1996 production Bad Day at Black Frog Creek. (Bryon Fear, 2015)

Opposite: School for Scandal, 1970. (SLT Archive)

CHAPTER FOURTEEN

Smoke and mirrors – the craft of backstage

As one of SLT's more prolific directors, Anton Krause is famous for saying that any production he directs "only needs a lightbulb and a chair. Two if absolutely necessary". SLT strives, with every production, to help a director achieve his or her vision in myriad different eras, styles and levels of complexity. From two chairs and a lightbulb (*Gagarin Way*, 2009), to revealing a mountainside Italian castle on the cusp of summer (*Enchanted April*, 2010), SLT's dedicated team is able to realise even the most fevered director's dream.

MEET THE CREW

The technical and backstage departments are headed by Chaz Doyle, who became the general stage manager in 2010.

"I love acting and directing, but there is something immensely satisfying about building a set, lighting it and crafting a soundscape that affects the actors and the audience. Essentially, creating the world for the actors on stage to inhabit," he says.

Although in charge of backstage, the role of the general stage manager is to facilitate and enable the membership when putting together a show. Every show needs set builders, lighting designers, operators, painters, etc, and SLT thrives because of its membership.

"I expect everyone in the cast and crew to turn up for the get-in and the get-out," Chaz continues. "Everyone can help, no matter what level of experience. If you've never used a power drill before, then we're happy to teach you. Even if we run out of jobs building the set, there are props to be sourced, costumes to be ironed, and as a last resort, the cast could even run their lines."

Opposite: Coils of rope from the fly loft are de-rigged and placed ready for storage. Behind them, rostra stage blocks are stacked ready to extend the front of the stage towards the audience. (Kate Monro)

Over the years SLT has put together a large collection of lighting fixtures, initially all designed to run from a 20-channel Strand dimmer. In the early 2000s, the lighting system was upgraded from the stolid Strand to a system of smaller satellite dimmer packs and moved on to a professional-level computer-based system, giving lighting designers more flexibility. With the recent advent of LED lighting, more professional theatres are replacing their old fixtures with new, cheaper to run, LED equivalents, and SLT is not far behind. As part of the restoration of the Old Fire Station, SLT will be a more green organisation, aiming to eventually move to a completely LED lighting rig.

Crafting the sound for a production is as important as lighting it. Old-school methods would include closing an actual door offstage for the sound effect, having a small group of carol singers ready in the wings, and even hitting the floor with a large stick to simulate a shotgun going off (*The Lonesome West*, 2009).

"Having the sound of the winter wind swirling around the audience is wonderful and can really draw them into the show, but if the sound of the phone ringing on stage doesn't come from the actual phone on the stage, then you break the spell and risk losing the audience," Chaz explains.

The sound system at SLT allows for some effective and immersive soundscapes, drawing the audience into the production and sometimes unnerving

Above: The backstage crew finish taking down a set. (Kate Monro)

them. All computer based, the software allows for timed cues, automatic fades, sweeping pans and much more. The system is also able to control the lighting software, making running a show a (sometimes) simple affair for the operator.

Recently the use of projections as a part of a production has become much more common. The West End production of *The Woman in White* in 2004 was famous for being the first show to use all projections for the set design. While SLT has not gone that far, projections have been used in many shows, from providing asteroid cloud simulations (*The Dust Collectors*, 2007) to a window to hell, where Hedda Hopper and Louella Parsons passed on acid-tongued critique to a dying Bette Davies (*Bette & Joan: The Final Curtain*, 2017).

Another crucial part of running a show is the backstage crew. Once the show is up, the director's job is done and it is now down to the actors on stage. Or so it seems to the audience. Headed up by a stage manager, the backstage crew is in charge of the show from dress rehearsal onwards. They make sure the cast is in place and ready to go from well before curtain up and possibly for each scene. They set and change the scenery, have the props ready, liaise with front of house and the show operator and ensure the production is consistent and perfect every night. SLT is fortunate to have several great stage managers, some of whom have worked professionally, and who are the backbone of every production.

"Every actor should help stage manage a show," says Chaz. "You learn so much about how a show works and what is required to keep it running smoothly. It is an invaluable part of stage craft."

SLT strives with every production to make it as professional a piece of theatre as possible, albeit with a very small budget. There is always space for someone who wants to help design, build or paint a set, design lights or sound, stage manage and much more.

Above: The stage manager of 2015's New Electric Ballroom waits backstage to hand an actor a tray of frozen fish. (Phil Gammon)

CHAPTER FIFTEEN

The Old Fire Station in the 21st century

The South London Theatre moved into the new century, much like everyone else, with a party. Televisions were rigged up in the bar and tuned to Big Ben and the South Bank. Once the Thames and the Millennium Wheel (as it was then named) had been doused down, members climbed the stairs and a mini firework display was held on the flat roof.

Productions continued as they had in the 20th century, commencing with Matthew Bartlett's *Much Ado About Nothing*, and swiftly followed by *Glengarry Glen Ross*, directed by Anton Krause, on the main stage, while *Dreamjobs* by Graham Jones and *The Disorderly Women*, John Bowen's updated telling of *The Bacchae*, kicked things off in Prompt Corner.

BUILDING PRESERVATION TRUST

After many years of trying to maintain an old building in desperate need of repairs, in the early 2000s the theatre began the long process of finding help, advice and funding to acquire the building and to get it restored and opened to the public. In 2006 the SLT Building Preservation Trust Ltd (BPT), a new charity, was formed to secure the funding and oversee the work necessary to restore the building to its former glory.

Bob Callender, a director of the building trust and one of the driving forces behind the refurbishment, explains: "The South London Theatre had managed some basic maintenance, but by the end of the 20th century the Old Fire Station was in serious decline. The front of the building was so shabby and run-down that passers-by thought it was abandoned. The roof space was infested with pigeons. Water was running in through broken tiles on the roof and making its way down inside the building and whenever it rained, a torrent gushed from a broken gutter to the back row of theatre

Opposite: The hand-painted sign that directed audience members to the theatre's entrance would prophetically point towards Stanley Halls, which would later become SLT's temporary home. (Kate Monro)

SOUTH
LONDON
THEATRE

seats. Sometimes water would run down the walls of the bar and often it would drip from the electrics of the lighting rig on to the main stage. Sometimes it would soak the ceilings and send chunks of plaster crashing to the floor."

It became harder to find companies willing to provide insurance, and without that cover the theatre would not be able to continue.

Then, in 2004, Lambeth Council announced that it was disposing of a series of buildings it owned, the Old Fire Station included. SLT would need either to fix it up and buy it, or leave. Some money had been saved, and the theatre had enough income to look after the building once it was restored, but the millions needed to perform a full restoration were beyond its resources.

"For more than 10 years we faced a long and repetitive process of meetings, plans, funding applications, rejections, then fresh meetings," Bob continues. "When we started, none of us on the BPT had any idea how to go about the task, but along the way we found many people and organisations willing to help us with time, money, advice and mentorship, including The Architectural Heritage Fund, English Heritage, The Victorian Society, The Heritage of London Trust, our local Lambeth councillors and officers and, of course, the Heritage Lottery Fund.

The road to funding was not an easy one. "Planning what the restored building would be like was a fraught process," Bob explains. "We needed to try to preserve the character of the theatre we all loved, but also make it accessible with a lift and up-to-date facilities. We needed to balance the need for a blank-canvas performance space with the need for a characterful, restored fire station where visitors could learn about the heritage of the building. Not long after we appointed him, our lead architect stood facing the darkened stage of the Bell Theatre and said, 'Look at this, you could be absolutely anywhere.' This was a lovely tribute for a theatre, but a bit of a clanger for a heritage attraction."

With the promise of restoration at hand, the insurance company allowed the building to stay on its books, and SLT was able to remain. During this time a good chunk of the income from ticket sales, membership subs, bar takings and costume

Above: Water damage had caused holes and weakened the structural fabric of the building by 2015. (Phil Gammon)

hire was poured into planning the restoration project. The theatre needed architects, quantity surveyors, project managers, acoustic consultants, theatre consultants, lawyers, heritage activity specialists, asbestos specialists, exhibition designers, mechanical and electrical engineers and fundraising specialists. And all these roles had to be tendered out, applicants interviewed and appointed, and payments made for their work.

Eventually, in 2014, the BPT received the news that its long, painstakingly planned and meticulously detailed major funding application was approved by the Heritage Lottery Fund (HLF). It would grant 70% of the £2.6 million needed. The theatre still had to provide match funding of more than £700,000, but with a robust plan and the HLF on board, other funders were more likely to see the project as viable.

"We set once again to fundraising, and accumulated grants from The Golden Bottle Trust, The John Horseman Trust, The Foyle Foundation and Garfield Weston Foundation, as well as some touchingly generous donations from members of the theatre themselves," Bob continues. "Lambeth Council agreed to extend us a loan facility of up to £250,000. This, combined with the £200,000 fighting fund we had managed to carefully preserve for the previous 10 years, meant that we could press ahead with appointing a lead building contractor and getting work started."

During the final months of 2015 the last productions were performed in the Old Fire Station as it stood, then the company packed up and moved to its temporary home at Stanley Halls in South Norwood. Final responses to the invitations to tender for the works were due to be received, but when the bids came back, the lowest price quoted was significantly higher than the budget allowed.

There followed a frantic period of to-ing and fro-ing between the architects, the contractor and the funding bodies. Could some of the costs be taken out of the plans? Could the contractor bring its prices down? Could more funding be raised at short notice? After a few tense weeks, agreement was reached, a start date was set, and sighs of relief were heaved.

Above: Many forgotten treasures were rediscovered during the clearout of 2015, such as an old operating desk. (Phil Gammon)

But things were about to take a nasty turn. Bob explains: "With just weeks to go until the start date, the winning contractor pulled out, leaving us high and dry. We found out later it was in serious financial trouble and went bust a few months afterwards."

So the process had to start again, looking for ways to save more money, examining the prices and requirements, returning to Lambeth Council to try to increase the loan, making sure the HLF would still fund the project if the scope was reduced, and making new applications to potential funders.

40TH ANNIVERSARY – 2007

Another milestone in the theatre's history, the South London Theatre hit 40 years old in 2007, and the anniversary was celebrated all year in a number of ways:

An anniversary brochure was produced that spanned every aspect of the theatre, from when it all started through to the anniversary. Forty years of productions were listed, and this was the forerunner of the theatre's Wiki archive website. Mention was made of plans for a major refurbishment, although it took a further decade for this to come to fruition.

The anniversary production in September was *Beautiful Thing* by Jonathan Harvey (*pictured above*). With the Bell stage transformed into a Thamesmead housing estate, the show focuses on the first love experienced by two teenage boys when their mutual attraction develops into sexual awakening.

A 40th-anniversary party, utilising the whole building, completed the year's celebrations on 19 November. Invitations were sent out to members past and present, and photographic displays of past productions and mini tours were on offer, to show how things had changed. With food and drink flowing until 2am, a successful evening was spent celebrating 40 years of SLT.

"This time, finally, we did it," says Bob. "In summer 2016 the moving parts came together and a last-minute injection of a £50,000 grant from the City Bridge Trust brought us to a relatively secure position. The builders moved in, the hoardings went up and the transformation of the building began."

By December 2016, there were still some wrinkles to iron out with the council and the HLF about the terms of the lease and the final specs of the building, while the theatre began work to appoint designers to bring together the exhibition that visitors to the new Old Fire Station will see on display.

"We're optimistic that there will be a rather attractive Victorian fire station, newly restored, fresh paint shining, front doors open to welcome visitors and some interesting things to look at, and somewhere inside, hidden away, a group of actors getting ready to put on a play," Bob concludes.

Above: The revival of Abigail's Party, 2015. (Phil Gammon)

DREAMS BECOME REALITY

When, in 2014, the necessary funding was granted and the green light was given to press ahead to appoint a building contractor, HLF gave notice that the theatre would have to vacate the Old Fire Station at the end of June 2015. Theatre Committee hastily came up with a modified six-month season that would cover January to June 2015. However, due to unforeseen financial issues, the departure date was put back to the end of October, giving the theatre an additional three months in the building.

The beginning of the season included five revivals: *Nunsense* (also 1993); *Abigail's Party* (also 1985); *Macbeth* (1977, 1980 and 2004); *Betrayal* (1993); and *The Accrington Pals* (1985).

The production of *Abigail's Party* happened exactly 30 years exactly after it was first performed and in this version was a brilliantly funny period piece, with a set, costume and music typifying the mid-1980s.

The Youth Theatre took its usual slot in February in the Bell Theatre while in June and July the theatre was opened to several well-known comedy acts trying out their pre-Edinburgh material, including Josh Widdecombe and Angela Barnes.

The Spank House by Jake Costello, in July, was another late addition. This semi-autobiographical piece was about his involvement with a criminal organisation in Barcelona, for which he was duly punished. After reforming, he wrote about his exploits and brought it to life on the stage, playing all the parts himself in a highly physical 65-minute performance.

No productions in August gave much-needed time to dispose of surplus items and pack up costumes, props, set-building and lighting equipment ready for the move to Stanley Halls. There were still three more productions to mount, however, before then. The first was *Joseph K* by Tom Basden, a slick, dark comic adaptation of Franz Kafka's *The Trial*, which included a final touch of tastefully performed nudity.

In September came *Festen* by David Eldridge. The action started in a hotel foyer in Denmark and ended with a dinner party, where a three-course hot meal was served at a dining table which stretched the entire width of the stage.

The swansong production in October achieved something never attempted previously in the theatre's history, which was to put on two plays in one night, one in each theatre. Edgar and Annabel by Sam Holcroft was performed first in Bell, and Kim Goldsmith delivered the last line ever to be spoken on the Bell stage, which was, "Thought

so". After the interval, the audience moved to Prompt Corner for *The Swan* by DC Moore, set in a rundown South London pub.

The following Saturday, 17 October, it was all hands on deck for the big move, ferrying the remaining contents of the building down to Stanley Halls, including lighting, costumes and props. This was followed by a party in the bar. Lots of friends were invited back for the final time, photographs were taken and the odd tear was shed.

On 24 October 2015 those that could make it gathered at the Old Fire Station one last time. The instructions were to leave a completely empty building for the contractors and so anything remaining was piled into a skip and left outside the big red doors, before handing over the keys to the refurbishment project managers.

Above: One of the building's quirky features, 2015 (Brian Fretwell)

Opposite: Members clear the theatre for building works, 2015 (Bryon Fear)

CHAPTER SIXTEEN

The rescue and restoration of a heritage treasure

At 9am on Monday, 12 September 2016 representatives of Camelot Europe handed the keys of the Old Fire Station to Matthew Cox, commercial director of Ash Contracting Ltd, the builders tasked with the restoration and build of the new theatre.

BEST-LAID PLANS

The restoration plan was beset with a litany of setbacks. Building works had been scheduled to start shortly after the building was emptied in October 2015, but the estimated budget for the project did not match the tenders received. A process of negotiation began with the winning contractor to reduce the costs in an attempt to match the funds that had been raised, a process which took several months. The Old Fire Station during this period stood empty and vulnerable and on 1 December the building was broken into. Within days SLT had contracted Camelot Europe to protect the site. Camelot adapted the bar kitchen and fitted a shower in the ladies toilet so that live-in guardians could occupy the building until building works could begin. This was supposed to be a temporary measure ...

A DEVASTATING BLOW

Months later, at the 49th Annual General Meeting, SLT's chair Lee Ridgeway had to deliver the news that the original contractor was pulling out of the project just three weeks before building works were finally due to begin. It was devastating. The project was now seven months behind schedule and without a contractor to undertake the work. The budget had also increased significantly, prompting an immediate need for urgent fundraising. The whole project was now in jeopardy.

Opposite: Removing the roof of the St Luke's 1927 extension was one of the first works undertaken. November 2016. (Bryon Fear)

PHOENIX FROM THE ASH

In August 2015, Ash Contracting Ltd rescued the project with an amended budget and proposed a plan of works which was approved by the Heritage Lottery Fund. Just five weeks later they were on site and working closely with the project's appointed architects, Thomas Ford and Partners.

The process began with a "soft strip" of any material not of historic interest. During this work the remains of original pavings from the stables were discovered in the area that would become the new backstage space. Original windows that ran the length of the building at the rear were also discovered. Asbestos was found both underneath the Bell Theatre's stage and below its auditorium, which had to be cleared before demolition work could commence. Within a month, the flat roof of the St Luke's extension above Prompt Corner had been removed exposing its original steelwork. A temporary staircase was erected for access from

the ground floor to the fly loft and the north-facing extension which had housed both the men's and women's conveniences was ripped away, returning the north aspect to its original shape.

Inside the building, which at this point was a mere shell, pits were being dug down into the ground to test the foundations, while above the ceiling that had been removed by SLTC in 1967 to create the fly loft was being infilled, creating a new floor and restoring the room that had once existed there.

RAISING THE ROOF

One of the most complex parts of the restoration was the creation of the new theatre space. The roof needed to be raised and the existing steel work replaced with six tonnes of new steel which would form the roof and a new stairwell for emergency

Above: The north extension is demolished. November 2015. (Bryon Fear)

access. Also, the south-west corner of the building was being supported by a column which needed to be moved by a metre to improve theatre flexibility and sight-lines in the new space. It was a massive undertaking which involved the building being propped up on 10 temporary posts while the column was repositioned.

DIGGING DOWN TO GO UP

The next phase of the project was to start the preparatory work so that a lift for accessibility could be installed. When digging the foundations in the members' bar the contractors discovered that the river Effra inconveniently flows below it. While work in the basement went down, scaffold on the exterior went up in February 2017, allowing access to the roof where masonry, tiles and leadwork were restored or replaced.

Above: Repositioned corner column (white). June 2017. (Bryon Fear)

Installation began in spring 2017 of a new plant room which would power and control the new heating system. Located on the flat roof on the north-west corner of the building, it can be seen from the street. It is a hot-air heating system which uses a set of air ducts to distribute heat throughout the building while a second set of ducts extracts to prevent the air from becoming stale.

At this time the steel framework was erected on the extension that faces the high street at the building's southern side. The blockwork (which can be seen top right corner in the photograph above) was constructed, ready for its polycarbonate façade.

PRESERVING THE PAST

Throughout the project, original features have been restored or reinstated where possible. For example, the brickwork's Victorian black pointing (mortar) was analysed and matched.

By June 2017 scaffolding began to come down around the building's iconic tower which had now been fully restored inside and out, with particular attention paid to its distinctive terracotta tiles.

In the stairwell, the 1920s alterations to lower levels of the 1881 stairs were stripped out and new timber flights were added to match the original pattern.

INTRODUCING THE NEW

It was one year into the project when the polycarbonate cladding went up on the new stairwell. The materials used for the extension were chosen specifically to emphasise the distinction between the fabric of the original building and its modern counterpart. Unlike the alterations made by Ernest Cole for St Luke's Church in the 1920s, which were designed to appear seamless, the architects for the restoration, Thomas Ford and Partners, wanted it to be clear where the old meets the new. Three entrances were created in the exterior wall connecting the main building with the new stairwell which traverses down the exterior southern wall.

Above left: The fire station's original Victorian range initialled with MFB (Metropolitan Fire Brigade) above its coal door, discovered during the restoration works. May 2018. (Bryon Fear)

Above right: Restored bannister in the stairwell. May 2018. (Bryon Fear)

Opposite: An artist's impression of the HLF-funded foyer artwork featuring images from past SLT productions. May 2018. (Bryon Fear)

The building shed its scaffold skin in late October revealing its rejuvenated masonry, sash windows and restored brickwork. Inside, timber suspended deck was constructed above existing and new slab floor to create a service void and a single ground floor level facilitating access for wheelchair use.

In the final months the building began to noticeably change on a daily basis with interior walls going up and the lift put in place. The basement bar was built while electrics, plumbing and security systems were installed. Acoustic separation works were undertaken in the theatre and foyer to provide a level of soundproofing to those spaces.

Then in March, a team of SLT members led by Chaz Doyle prepared the new theatre, painting the ceiling, the walls and the floor black. They rigged a lighting grid and hung lamps ready for the first show.

On 20 March, 2018 the inaugral production in the new space, Philip Pullman's *His Dark Materials* adapted by Nicholas Wright took place, performed by the SLT Youth Theatre. The production sold out as friends, family and the local community came together to celebrate the return of the theatre and the reopening of a much-loved building.

The Old Fire Station was restored. Its original entrance, the majestic double red fire doors, were ready once again to invite visitors inside to discover the rich history of its fascinating past and to enjoy its future as a thriving theatre and community space.

Above: Inside the new black box theatre space. The modular seating can be configured in a variety of ways creating an exciting and wholly adaptable performace space. March 2018 (Bryon Fear)

Opposite: The Old Fire Station restored. The red brick Victorian splendour married with its modern extension. May 2018 (Bryon Fear)

BIBLIOGRAPHY

Books, reports, brochures, newspapers & magazines

BOOKS

Beatti, Susan, (1980), *A Revolution in London Housing, LCC Architects and Their Work*, The Greater London Council in Association with The Architectural Press Ltd

Coulter, John, (1996), *Norwood Past*, London, Historical Publications Ltd

Coulter, John, (2012), *Norwood: A Second Selection*, Stroud, The History Press

Lambert, F D, Holdaway, K R, Lambert M D, (1974), *St Luke's, West Norwood 1825-1975*, London, London Borough of Lambeth

Jackson, W Eric, (1966), *London's Fire Brigades*, London, Longmans

Kenyon, John, (1914), *Fires and Firefighters*, London, Heinemann, Huddersfield, Jeremy Mills Publishing Ltd

Nadal, John B, (2006), *London's Fire Brigades*, Huddersfield, Jeremy Mills Publishing Ltd

Reading, Will, (2010), *London's Historic Fire Stations, EH and LFB Joint Guidance*, Swindon, English Heritage

Wilson, J B, (1990), *The Story of Norwood*, London, The Norwood Society

REPORTS

Butti, K, (2013), *Conservation Plan, South London Theatre, Old Fire Station, Norwood*, London, Thomas Ford & Partners

BOOKLETS & BROCHURES

London Fire Brigade Museum, *Captain Shaw and the Metropolitan Fire Brigade*

South London Theatre Centre, (1977), *10th Anniversary brochure 1967-1977*

South London Theatre Centre, (1992), *25th Anniversary brochure 1967-1992*

South London Theatre, (2007), *40th Anniversary brochure 1967-2007*

South London Theatre Centre Newsletters, (1967-1976)

South London Theatre Tour Guides, (2008-2014), for annual Open House events

NEWSPAPERS & MAGAZINES (references also given in footnotes and text)

The Metropolitan Fire Brigade: Its Home and its work, (1891, vol 1, issue 1, January), *Strand Magazine*, p 22, (ch 1, p 6)

'A bogus fire brigade' (1892, 26 May), *Lancashire Evening Post* p 4 (ch 1, p 14)

'West Norwood' (1887, 24 September), *Croydon Advertiser and East Surrey Reporter*, p 3 (Albert Cottages fire, ch 1, p 17 in box)

'A railway bridge on fire' (1887, 17 May) *Nottingham Evening Post*, p 3 (ch 1, p 17 in box)

'Penge: A Fire' (1891, 4 July), *Croydon Advertiser and East Surrey Reporter*, p 7 (Three brigades fire at Borrowdale, ch 1, p 17 in box)

'Untitled', (1892, 26 September), *London Evening Standard*, p 6 (Furniture Depository Burnt Out, ch1, p 17)

"Water jets for extinguishing fires", (1877, 6 July), *Building News and Engineering Journal*, p 5 (Report to Metropolitan Fire Brigade select committee by Joseph Bazelgette, ch 1, p18)

'Fire!', (1898, 24 December), *Croydon Advertiser and East Surrey Reporter*, p 7 (ch 1, p 18)

'Fires in London', (1898, 9 April), *London Daily News*, p 8 (Nursery fire! ch 1, p 18)

'Gallant Rescues by Firemen Want of Water' (1899, 4 March), *Croydon Advertiser and East Surrey Reporter*, p 7 (Destructive Fire at Upper Norwood, ch 1, p18-20)

'Commercial and Markets' (1900, 14 August), *London Daily News*, p 2 (Shocking Paraffin Lamp fatality! ch 1, p 20)

'Fire to Dulwich College: A Timely discovery', (1913, 6 September) *Yorkshire and Leeds Intelligencer*, p 10 (ch 1, p 21)

"A report on West Norwood Fire Station by Chief Fire Officer, James de Courcy Hamilton, 1908, 2 December", quoted in Butti, K, (2013), *Conservation Plan, South London Theatre, Old Fire Station, Norwood*, London, Thomas Ford and Partners (ch 1, p 26)

'It is proposed to erect a new fire station at West Norwood at a cost of £13,777', (1914, 28 July), *Surrey Mirror*, p 3 (New Fire Station for West Norwood, ch 1, p 26)

Brown, Edwin G and Wallace, Mike, (1999), *Gotham: A History of New York City to 1898* p 660 quoted at: http://glassian.org/Prism/Hyatt/index/html (accessed 22 April 2018), ch 2, p 34

Madgwick, D, (11 Feb1977), 'Review of Agamemnon', *Croydon Advertiser*, (ch 5, p 53)

LMA P85/LUK/101 St Luke's West Norwood Church Council Minute book 1917-1924 quoted in Butti, K, (2013), *Conservation Plan, South London Theatre, Old Fire Station, Norwood*, London, Thomas Ford and Partners (from St Luke's Church Council Minutes 1917-1924, ch 1, p 27)

LMA P85/LUK/101 St Luke's West Norwood Church Council Minute book 1917-1924 quoted in Butti, K, (2013), *Conservation Plan, South London Theatre, Old Fire station, Norwood*, London, Thomas Ford and Partners (from St Luke's Church Council Minutes 1917-1924, ch 1, p 27)

ST LUKE'S CHURCH NEWS – ST LUKE'S, WEST NORWOOD PARISH MAGAZINES

LMA P85/LUK/109 –144, *St Luke's Church News* 1917-1963, and LMA P85/LUK/131 – 140 1950-1959 (ch 2-3, p 28-39)

LMA P85/LUK/109, *St Luke's Church News*, 1917 (ch 2, p 28, 30)

LMA P85/LUK/110, *St Luke's Church News*, Jan 1928, Vicar of St Luke's Church (ch 2, p 34)

LMA P85/LUK/141, Oct 1960, LMA P85/LUK/143, Jan 1962, LMA P85/LUK/144, Oct 1963, all quotes from Dr Francis, *St Luke's Church News* (ch 2, p 38, 39, 40)

LMA P85/LUK/127, *St Luke's Church News*, 1946, Church Hall Accounts for 1946 (ch 2, p 39)